YOU CAN OVERCOME ANYTHING

EVEN WHEN THE WORLD SAYS "NO"

CESAR R. ESPINO

Hi Eddie,

Thank you so much for the love & support. I am grateful for our connection. I know you will enjoy this read & find at least "one" thing to inspire you 😊

7/9/19   VALENTINE BOOKS

Published by Valentine Books.

You Can Overcome Anything / Cesar R. Espino — 1st ed.

ISBN 978-1-64184-096-5 (dBook)
ISBN 978-1-64184-088-0 (pbk)

www.c2realestateinvestments.com

DISCLAIMER

Some names and identifying details have been changed to protect the privacy of individuals.

I have tried to recreate events, locales, and conversations from my memories of them. In order to maintain their anonymity, in some instances I have changed the names of individuals and places. I may also have changed some identifying characteristics and details such as physical properties, occupations, and places of residence.

FOREWORD

Why did I write this book, and who is this book for?

The answer can be found throughout the lessons and experiences described herein. In its simplest form, this book was written for everyone who has faced or is facing challenges that seem impossible to overcome.

Within these pages, you will find real-life examples of what I have faced as well as how I was able to continue to rise above even when all the signs around me were pulling me down, telling me I couldn't become anything more than I was.

While I did not have the choice of whether or not to come into this world or be born into a wealthy family, I did have a choice when it came to what my future would look like. Every day, many people only accept what they see, and do not seek a better future. Even when they do, they tend to give up when there is no sign of results. A lot of times, the moment when people are ready to give up, the answer is just around the corner.

Life tends to put forth so many obstacles and challenges, and it is up to us never to give up and always keep seeking. After all, life will happen regardless of what we believe. There is, however, one thing we can do to challenge life and make a change, and that is accept that for our own life to change, we have to take action. We have to do something to change our inner life so that our outer life can change.

As you read this book, you will find that the one thing I did not ever do is give up, regardless of my background, my ethnicity, my many challenges, and my acquaintances. Not only did I not give up, I reinvented myself through continuous education, training, and people.

Why is education so important? Because it is the foundation of understanding how to do something rather than not knowing and doing nothing about the situation at all. It is also important to recognize the different types of education available, and as you will learn, in order to win in any aspect of your life, you must engage in the right type of education. Equally important is that you spend time with people who are going to lift you up rather than bring you down. The type of associations you have day-to-day will determine where you will end up.

Finally, as you read this book, you are likely going to come to the realization that you need to make changes and go through a transformation of your own if you are going to succeed and stay afloat from this point forward. I encourage you to put into practice some of the things that are reviewed in this book, and above all, do not stop fighting. This means do not stop your discipline, do not stop enhancing your mind, do not allow fear to overtake your capabilities, and do not stop in your effort to get the freedom and life you want.

To be rich and wealthy inside and out, you need to be at peace with yourself and everyone else

"You need to associate with people who inspire you, people that challenge you to raise higher, people that make you better. Don't waste your valuable time with people that are not adding to your growth. Your destiny is too important."
—*Joel Osteen*

PART I

0 TO 10

DON'T LET SOCIETY SHIFT YOUR FOCUS

Oftentimes as individuals we have a false vision of what it is within our reach as well as what we are capable of doing for ourselves. For many, not understanding the options and only accepting what society seems to offer is a major obstacle to overcome. The problem is, they don't know how. Illustrating my life story and challenges is intended to provide the vision that there is more to life than we think.

My story is just a vehicle to provide you with inspiration, tools, and guidelines to create actions that will shift your focus as soon as you recognize and understand that there is no better time to take action than *now*. Although this is my story, and the story that truly matters is yours, I hope you will allow my experiences to empower you to be whomever you want to be and do whatever you want to do.

In his book, *The Miracle Morning*, Hal Elrod says, "We must embrace the fact that if we don't commit to thinking and living differently than most people now, we are setting ourselves up to endure a life of mediocrity, struggle, failure, and regret—just like most people."

I was born in Mexico City on January 27, 1980, into a country with the world's largest foreign debt. Not only was I born into a poor family, I also came into this world during a time when Mexico was experiencing a major financial crisis. As were many families in my community, we were less than fortunate, living in a place made out of sheet metal, just large enough at 200 square feet to hold a family of four. This place we called home was not my family's place. We rented it. We had no floor or insulation (we lived and slept directly on dirt), and we had no inside running water (we had to get water from a faucet outside), yet it was enough for my family. Rather, my family did not know better and chose to accept these conditions as livable.

Not only was I born into a corrupt society, I was also born to just one parent (the father's section on my original birth certificate is blank). Even now, I have no clue who my biological father is (I've never bothered asking my mom about him—his name or his background. I know absolutely nothing). He did not want me to come into this world, and just that reality made my childhood more challenging. Since I didn't have a biological father, my mom decided to give me her last name (the last name given to her from her father, Merced Espino). In Mexican culture (as in many Latin-American countries) I had a second last name, and the one given to me was my grandma's first last name. Her name is Esperanza Martinez, and as such I was named Cesar Espino Martinez.

I was raised by my mother and my grandmother (my mother's mom) and grew up with a brother who is two years older. At that time, the life given to me was just another day in poverty, and in many aspects, the days to come would be full of struggle for survival. Growing up, the dream that "you can be anything you want when you grow up" was far from reality. Looking back, I've realized that as a toddler, I did not have too many options, and the life I lived was the only life known to me. There are always choices, except when the society and environment you are born into puts a blindfold over your eyes, taking away the endless possibilities this world has to offer. Sometimes, those choices are outside your reach or outside of what you are capable of, and someone else who cares for you will seek to get you there so you may realize the greatness you can become.

> "There is no exercise better for the heart than reaching down and lifting people up."
> ——*John Holmes*

I am grateful my loving mother and grandma came to realize that, after so much struggle and worry, we all deserved a better tomorrow. But it wasn't an easy dream for any of us to follow.

On May 3, 1984, my mother decided to make a temporary sacrifice and leave her family behind to chase the American dream. This was the year my mom left Mexico, her mom, my older brother, and me (only three months after I turned four years old) to pursue a better future for us, not knowing if it would ever work or know when we would again be reunited as one family. From this point forward, my life changed. This marked the beginning of hard work while living with my older brother and grandma, never having met my father, and no longer having a mother, who I slowly learned to forget. Perhaps one of the hardest things for me to overcome (more about this later) was living with the thought that my own mother left me behind and not understanding as a child why my mom did this to me or to my family.

Looking back, finding my mother's letter, which was addressed to my grandma, puts things into a different perspective and only validates that, many times, there is a person in your life who wishes for only the best for you. It could be your wife, your husband, brother, mother, father, or friend. For me, it was my mother. Finding this letter in my adult years illustrated that I was not the only one suffering. On the other side, close to the US border, I had a mother ready to cross over into a new country, a new world, to chase the dream. Her purpose for working day-in and day-out was to provide and give to our family while being away from home. Also, she was working for what she was not able to give and provide for us in our own country.

This goes to show that there are many societies (countries) that do not create possibilities that allow their citizens to provide for their families, regardless of the type of education they have. Unfortunately, many of these countries have broken systems and only favor a certain group of people. Mexico is a country that clearly classifies its own citizens into different groups and class levels (known as the Mexico Social Hierarchy), and if you are not in the right class, your challenge is really only your challenge, not that of the government. Especially for the lowest class in the hierarchy (to which my family and I belong), in its simplest form, money and power are the key driving factors for social classification.

Considering that my family and I were in the bottom of the social hierarchy, we had to improvise to survive. This was the beginning of a new stage in my life. With no father or mother around, I had to grow up rather quickly and let my childhood years pass by me without ever experiencing them. During this time, all I knew was that, from that point forward, there were only three of us, and this new family (made up of my grandma, older brother, and myself) was all we had. I learned to love both my grandma and older brother, and for as long as I can remember, we were inseparable.

My grandma was a firm believer in education, and because of her beliefs, she made sure that my older brother and I went to school. Regardless of her situation, it was important to her for us to get educated, because her belief was that with an education I could get a good job. Although during the day, I was just like any other kid— going to school, playing during recess and lunch—after school, I was a different kid.

To an extent, you could say I was a young adult, forced by my living conditions to become responsible and a man at an early age. After school, I had to work to help my family survive for that day. My grandma would bake cookies and bread, and my older brother and I would assist. We helped out by preparing and stirring the flour, kneading dough, rolling the dough, creating the cookie shapes, and making different bread shapes. Not only did we bake bread and cookies, we also had a cookie and bread stand near my elementary school in a *tianguis* (flea market), where we would go daily to make a living by selling our bread.

This was not enough to survive, so we had to do other things and offer other things for sale. Aside from cookies and bread, we began to sell tacos, quesadillas, and homemade *obleas* (wafers). This was a time of real struggle, with many challenges to face, yet the three of us would do this day-in and day-out with a smile, faith, and gratitude that we had the opportunity to sell and bring in just enough to survive. Don't get me wrong, there were days when we didn't make any profit or even close to the amount of money we spent for the day. However, one thing was for sure, and that was that my grandma was a true hero, a woman with strength and perseverance who never gave up on providing just enough for us.

> "Always bear in mind that your own resolution to succeed is more important than any one thing."
> —*Abraham Lincoln*

My grandma was always a fighter, and she always looked at ways to improve our living situation. This, of course, brought about more challenges, and before I go into detail on those challenges, I want to take you back to 1986.

On October 10, 1986, my grandma wrote a letter and sent it to the Delegate of Tlahuac to plead for help. The letter was simple yet very powerful, asking for permission to allow her to build a humble home of two bedrooms and a kitchen in an empty lot that her husband (my grandpa, who I never met) had left her.

Part of the letter read:

"Le suplico tenga a bien concederme el permiso para hacer en el terreno que me compró mi difunto esposo unos dos cuartos y una cocina, terreno de mi propiedad ubicado en la calle de Narciso Villarroel Cruz entre la calle de Violeta y Calle Azucena, Manzana 8 Lote uno, colonia Quiahuatla."

Translation:

I beg you to give me permission to build on the lot that my deceased husband bought for me, two rooms and a kitchen, the land of my property located in the street of Narciso Villarroel Cruz between the street Calle of Violeta and Calle Azucena, Manzana 8 Lote (lot) uno (one), Colonia Quiahuatla.

And it goes on to say: *"Pues yo y mis pequeños nietos*

huérfanos de padre, vivimos en una situación precaria e insalubre, pues los techos y paredes son de carton y pedazos de madera y estamos enfermos de los bronquios, ya que el asfalto llegó a solo 40 metros aproximadamente de distancia de mi casa."

Translation:

For me and my young grandchildren, orphans of a father, we live in a precarious and unhealthy situation, because the ceilings and walls are of cardboard and pieces of wood, and we are sick of bronchitis since the asphalt reaches approximately only forty meters of distance to my house.

My grandma finished her letter by stating, *"Señor delegado por lo que le suplico tenga bien concederme el permiso, por lo que le estaré eternamente agradecida, pidiéndole a Dios que lo bendiga, y estará usted seimpre en mis oraciones."*

Translation:

Mr. Delegate, for what I implore you to grant me permission, I will be eternally grateful to you, asking God to bless you, and you will be always in my prayers.

With much persistence, faith, and love, the delegate granted my grandma the permission to build the house. Shortly after, we moved to this land. First, we built a small room made out of cardboard, sheet metal, and wood right on the dirt ground with no running water and no electricity for the three of us while we saved money to build a more solid house (two rooms and a kitchen).

"I have learned over the years that when one's mind is made up, this diminishes fear."

—*Rosa Parks*

2

WORKING HARD PAYS OFF

The year was 1987. Up to this point, my childhood had been that of a working child, allowing no time to play like other children from my block. We didn't have birthday parties or celebrations, presents, or even decent clothes. All I'd known up to this point was the life of a poor boy. Until the unexpected happened.

My mom, who by this time I had not seen for over three years, was coordinating with my grandma to have us come to the US. After what seemed like an eternity, she actually worked to have us travel from Mexico City to Tijuana in order for us to cross over into the US and reunite with her. My mom did not have her documentation and was not able to leave the US or else she would have to re-enter illegally, which was risky, as she was in the process of getting her legal status in the US.

It was June of 1987 when my mom had saved enough money to have all of us reunited with her on the other side. Soon after, she left us, and at the time, I did not understand it, however she left us with a particular purpose. As Jim Rohn said, "Your life does not get better by chance. It gets better by change." That was the kind of change and decision that my mother made when she migrated to the US and left us behind (with no hope or real purpose in my mind at that time). To our surprise, my mom had saved enough money to take the three of us to the US. American Dream, here we come! Or, at least, for a second I thought that. Just as fast as she sent for us, we were fast moving and experiencing something I never thought I would experience, and that is leaving Mexico City without ever thinking it would be possible, on our way to Tijuana, Mexico (via an airplane, for the first time ever).

Talk about crossing the border! During this time, the US's border patrol was lighter than it is now, and we did not have the proper documentation that was key to our successful travel into the new world. During the previous three years, and with the help of my mom's partner, they saved enough money to pay a *coyote* (human smuggler) to help us migrate to the US. It is unbelievable what an American Dream will do for you and those who love you as well as the amount of money needed to pay a coyote to do this type of smuggling job.

My mom paid a fee of $500 per person. Back in those days there were some coyotes who were more trustworthy, and my mom and her partner did not have to worry about any financial obligation until after we all crossed over to our final destination in the US. Sadly, the reality is that there are all kinds of coyotes. Some are good people, and some do not care and only worry about the money, not your wellbeing, during this type of experience. To our good luck, we had a great coyote on our side.

Just to put things into perspective, immigration is by far one of the major challenges the US has to face, not just from Mexico but also from all over the world. During the 1980s, around the time the three of us were crossing over illegally (1987), the US was providing housing to over two million unauthorized immigrants throughout the US. This figure went through the roof in 2007 to 11.78 million, and more recently, in 2016, the figure went to a whopping 11.3 million. If you were born here and are wondering why so many people leave their countries, chasing the American Dream, it is simple to write yet difficult to understand. Many other countries do not have the possibilities that this country has to offer due to corruption, poverty, limitations on the citizens, and unfair wages, which were the reasons my mom left us behind for a better tomorrow.

"Everything that is done in this world is done by hope."
——*Martin Luther*

I still vividly remember crossing into the US. Only the three of us (my grandma, my older brother, and I) and the one coyote had the mission to be in the "land of opportunity" that very same day. The only separation between one world and the other was the border, and what wasn't known was what the day had in store for us, whether we would reunite with my mom that same day. Even with those unknowns, with the coyote's determination and promise to have us in the US the same day we left Mexico, we began our journey.

We walked for miles during the night through the mountains, ducking and hiding in the bushes as the border patrol's helicopter was doing its normal routine, flashing its lights toward the ground. Thinking about it now reminds me of those movies when you see people running and hiding for safety. As funny as that may sound or seem, that was exactly what it was like. This was not as bad as the next challenge, where we had to cross a running river while it was dark and cold. Given my age and size, and not knowing how to swim, I had to be carried across the river. One might say this was our struggle in pursuing our dream. Yet, at my age, or even my older brother's age, we were just taken. We did not have the option to stay behind. At the end, this particular journey paid off.

Once we crossed over the mountains and river, we were able to reach a place where we had to stay overnight due to heavy immigration security in the San Clemente area. The next day, with little inspection we were taken into a car, and all I can remember is driving for a long period of time. By the time I woke up, I remember being in my mom's arms.

The drive was long because, as a foreigner never having been in California, I had no clue where we were going. The coyote took us from San Diego to his residence in Santa Ana, where my parents came to pick us up and took us to their residence in Los Angeles. Once you think about it, this experience was actually not painful after all, and on the other side, there was hope.

This was officially my first visit to the US, more specifically to Los Angeles, California, and I literally went from not having a family to having a full family (a mom, a stepdad, a grandma, and an older brother). From living in poverty and under unsafe housing conditions to what seemed to me to be a luxury house (although it was lower-class here in the US, it was glamorous compared to my living conditions in Mexico). To having nice clothes (matching clothes with my older brother) and really, a fairytale life compared to what I had experienced the previous seven years. It was breathtaking, unbelievable, hard to explain—that feeling when one day you literally have nothing, and you're working just to survive, and then the next day, you have everything and don't have to work and for the very first time. For the first time, you have time to play, be a kid (something I never was or had), and have nothing to worry about.

This experience was a dream, something I never could have imagined. My mom and stepdad made sure we had the best time of our lives. We went to almost every theme park in Southern California. We had adventures from Knott's Berry Farm to Disneyland to Universal Studios to Six Flags Magic Mountain. They ensured that we had an unbelievable experience. We went to more theme parks in just two months than many living in Southern California have gone to their entire lives.

"Remember to celebrate milestones as you prepare for the road ahead."
–Nelson Mandela

Interestingly, this was, unfortunately, just a dream of sorts, because our stay in the US was only temporary, even after making the sacrifice to cross over illegally. As a matter of fact, to this day, I still do not know why we couldn't stay forever, why it was just a temporary experience that lasted only two months. Nevertheless, during this time my older brother and I had the type of life that never could have imagined beforehand—a loving family, no worries, food (many days in Mexico we had nothing to eat), shoes, clothes, toys, and much more. You could say I was spoiled in the sense that the society I was born into had a different type of "spoiled;" this new, temporary life, this new society, gave me over ten times more than I had.

It is amazing how one's life can change drastically in any direction in just a matter of days; I know this for a fact because I lived it. At that time, it did not make sense. Now, as a grown man, it means so much. As John F. Kennedy said, "Children are the world's most valuable resource and its best hope for the future." I believe my mom had a vision of faith for what my older brother and I would become, and this was just part of the overall journey.

Can you imagine having the best dream of your life and then, all of a sudden, you are woken up and taken back to your previous reality? Let me tell you, it's not an easy feeling. In just the blink of an eye, in one overnight sleep, you find yourself packing and getting ready to go back to your previous life. The dream was taken back by real life, and my journey of joy ended.

Just as fast as we got to the US from Mexico, we were back to our old reality once we got back. Life was the same each and every day, except it was unlike any ritual or discipline practiced by many millionaires nowadays. The daily routine was more of a survival tactic, and it was as simple as this: wake up early, get ready for school, attend school, get home from school (when we could not go out and hang with friends), do our homework, eat whatever we had (there were many days we had no food, when all we had to eat was the Mexican specialty dish, a tortilla with some grains of salt, rolled in the form of a taco,) work, pray, and go to sleep. And then get up and do it again the next day.

By this time, we had graduated from selling quesadillas, tacos, and bread at a food stand. My grandma was able to get a contract with a doll toy factory about an hour away from the house, and our new job was to sew doll clothing. At one point, the three of us had our own sewing machines, and we were paid based on volume. Sometimes, we'd all work at the sewing machines together, putting clothes together until late into the night. Other times, we'd take turns. While my grandma sewed on the sewing machine, I would take care of thread cutting on the clothes for a clean presentation, and my older brother would fold the clothes inside out and prepare them for delivery. We'd then alternate positions.

I remember that our objective was to get the orders finished as quickly as possible. The faster we could get it done, the faster we could get paid. Since the company was far from the house, we had to deliver the clothes in large plastics bags, and given that we never had a car, we had to take the cheapest method of transportation to cut back on cost: *el camion*, the bus. We took the bus caring these huge plastic bags. Thank God we were never robbed.

3

SECOND CHANCES

L ife was not easy, yet it was satisfying, and because of my grandma's teaching, discipline, and perseverance, my older brother and I were known by the community as two great, hardworking, well-mannered kids. Much of this was a result of the fact that we did not have a choice; we had to grow up rather quickly in order to make ends meet.

Because of my experience, I do not believe that my struggle and way of growing up—not being able to be a kid—is something I would ever support or condone for any other child in this world. It is unfortunate that our world has many countries and economies that allow their citizens to suffer, forcing families like mine to have every member of the family working in order to survive. Although I sometimes wish my life as a child had been different, I wouldn't change the experience because it allowed me to become the man I am today. I share my life with you to encourage you, inspire you, and deliver the message that anything and everything is possible. As Tony Robbins has said, "The only impossible journey is the one you never begin."

As a kid, life was not easy, yet it was joyful because I learned to build disciplines, the hunger to do more, and the ability to work hard to obtain anything I want, and therefore so appreciate what I have today. As a kid, God gave me another opportunity at this life (my life), as I was on the verge of death at one point. Based on the doctors' feedback, I was just a day from leaving this world, and I am grateful to be here. Always be grateful to the higher power you believe in for what you have, regardless of where you are in your life.

At that time, we were still living in a house made out of wood and sheet metal with dirt floors. The days were cold, and not having the right shelter and clothes, I came down with a chronic cold and Typhoid Fever. Not having the money or means to go see a doctor, my grandma decided to treat my illness on her own (as many Mexican moms would do).

Day One went by, and I was not getting any better. Day Two went by, and I was still not getting any better. It did not matter what she gave me to kill the virus, it did not work. With my really high temperature and a lack of any improvement, my grandma decided to take me to the *Cruz Roja* (Red Cross) to have me checked out by the doctor. To our surprise, this was God's blessing, because it literally saved my life.

The doctor was very upset and angry at my grandma and scolded her. He clearly told her that if she would have waited one more day, she would have buried me instead of healing me. That day, I spend several hours at the doctor, I was subjected to an ice-cold shower in a tub to bring down my high temperature, and then I was further treated and released to get additional rest. Talk about a scare. I do believe that we all have second chances, and as I reflect on my life now, I strongly believe that this second chance was given to me so that I could find my true purpose and make an impact in this life. You only live once, and as long as you are still breathing, make the best of it. Work not only on yourself but also to improve the lives of those around you.

"If you are still breathing, you have a second chance."
—*Oprah Winfrey*

As the months and years went by, my life was still the same, living day to day, working, and growing older. It was the first half of 1990, and by this time I was ten years old. When my mom came back, it had been one and a half years since I'd last seen her—my parents had come once during Christmas to visit us after my mom received her residence card from the US. I was excited yet a bit confused at the same time. This time around, my mom did not come by herself; she came with a small boy who had just turned one. This little boy happened to be the new addition to the family and my new brother. Not a whole lot went through my mind except that I was no longer the youngest; I was suddenly the middle child.

I still remember a few months before my mom came to Mexico. I knew she was coming, and I would go to school and talk to my friends, telling them that my mom was coming from the US to take me to the other side. In fact, I might even be leaving for good. It was interesting to hear my classmates' and friends' perspectives of the American Dream. On top of that, it actually felt kind of good to say that I had the opportunity to leave Mexico and have a better life (that now seems perhaps a bit selfish on my part, given the others' circumstances).

As soon as my mom arrived, she took care of so many

things, such as settling my older brother's and my affairs at school, getting our dental work done (which had never been done given that we never had the money for it) as well as other affairs that she and my grandma took care of to get us ready to leave Mexico for our next chapter in life. Even at this point, it was surreal, because I knew I was leaving, and although I was told we were not coming back, in the back of my mind we had left once for just a few months before and then came back. So the reality of this being a permanent move was not fully hitting.

A new journey began, a new beginning, and even with the type of life I had, it was hard to leave everything and everyone behind—friends, acquaintances, the only life we knew. The only satisfaction I felt was that, in the end, those who I really knew and grew up with (my grandma and older brother) were going with me on this journey. We were truly inseparable as we worked, suffered, and survived together. The three of us went through so much suffering, and although my mom was sending my grandma financial support, the three of us were the ones who faced so much while living in Mexico.

For me, that was so important, since all I knew at that point was my grandma and older brother, no one else. Although I had an awesome time the first time I visited the US and I knew it was a better place, I also knew that the first time I went as a visitor. This time that wasn't the case, and I didn't know what to expect as an outsider. And then, just like that, I was leaving my neighborhood for a new dream and a new life, and the journey began from Mexico City as we made our way up to the border of Tijuana and the US to prepare to cross over.

A NEW CHAPTER

I ronically here we were again (my grandma, older brother, and I), along with a coyote, waiting for the right time to cross over to the US. This time around, it was not the same coyote as it was three years before, and the border patrol was much heavier, which meant that it was going to be much harder to get to the other side. This time around, my mom found this particular coyote via my dad's uncle, and the cost she paid for us to make it to the other side was $750 per person. We were not the only three people crossing with him as we were the first time; this time around there were at least ten of us, from what I can remember.

Due to heavy border patrol, once we crossed the border, the coyote had to take us to a motel room (what I would now recognize as a town before San Clemente, the second border patrol check point on the I-5 freeway). Upon our arrival to this motel room, we recognized that there were already easily fifteen or so people there. We were told to wait there for a few hours until the patrolling was reduced. The wait ended up not being only a few hours; it was actually days before we were able to leave. During our stay in this motel room, we were not able to see the light of day, we were not given adequate food and water, and younger females were raped by the same coyotes who were supposed to protect and help us. It was hard to tolerate, yet we had no other options, and all we could do was wait and thank God that nothing happened to my grandma or brother.

About seven days later, the day finally came when patrol and security was at its lowest point. The coyote finally got everyone out of the motel room. I still remember them trying to get all of us on the flatbed of a pickup truck, and I clearly remember my older brother and I telling the coyote that there was no way my grandma (at sixty-eight years old) was going to be able to lie flat and endure a long drive just lying there. We demanded that she be able to ride in the front cabin. By the grace of God, the coyote heard us and allowed my grandma to ride in the front while we went on the back with the others covered with sheets. This was our ride all the way to our final destination, and after a long drive, which was about two hours (but felt far longer), we arrived at a house late at night where my mom and her husband (who is now officially recognized as my father) arrived to pick us up.

Even with the struggle and bad experience, we arrived to our final destination, and it was the beginning of a new chapter, a new journey, and I again realized that this experience was one more test for me to show the world that I would eventually win—that no matter the struggles, no matter the negativity in this world, I would surpass my past, adjust to the new world, and come out achieving more than my original potential. I was born into challenging circumstances, but I was also born a winner.

"The road to success is through commitment and through the strength to drive through that commitment when it gets hard. And it is gonna get hard and you're gonna wanna quit sometimes, but it'll be colored by who you are, and more who you want to be."
— *Will Smith*

PART II

THE ADOLESCENT YEARS

5

NEW CULTURE

I n July 1990, my life started all over again. This was the year when I went from living in Mexico to being an illegal immigrant in the US. It was my first year being part of an unknown society. Not only did the Los Angeles Unified School District make me repeat the fifth grade (which I had finished in Mexico), and because of my age, they could not put me in sixth grade. On top of that, the US does not necessarily recognize two last names, so for the first time, my identity to others was simply Cesar Espino. I knew that, from that point forward, Martinez was no longer part of my identity. This was actually not the hardest part of the transition. The most difficult part was that my best friend and partner in crime (my older brother) was not enrolled in the same school as I was; he was enrolled in middle school.

Aside from not having my older brother near me throughout the day, I was inserted into a school where I knew no one, and for the first time in my life, I was in a class where one hundred percent of the students (as well as the teacher) spoke only English (a few students spoke

Spanish, yet it was rare). On top of that, there were different ethnicities such as African-American, Mexican-American, Asian-American, white, and Hispanic, which I wasn't used to and hadn't experienced before. In Mexico, the only language spoken was Spanish, and the only race/ethnicity I saw was Mexicans. Never in my life had I commingled with any other race, not even when I was in the US the first time. Although I'd been in the US, we were not commingling with anyone besides our direct family.

Fitting into a new life, a new society, a new classroom full of strangers who cannot understand you is just not easy, and it took me about a month to start talking to some of the students from my class. I was a victim of society, and many times I doubted whether or not my mom's decision to come to the US was the right one. My mom was not facing what I was facing. There were not only issues related to not fitting in, there was also discrimination. I had other classmates saying things to me, yet I could not understand any of it (I did not know a single word in English). I felt like I was not fit for this new life until deep down I decided not to be a victim and instead, be a victor. Shortly thereafter, I started talking to my bilingual classmates. Little by little, I begun somehow communicating with classmates who only spoke English.

Finally, after five or six months, I was in a different place at school and had learned to fit in as much as possible. My fifth grade teacher and I shared the same birthday (January 27th), and I remember when my teacher grabbed me, lifted me up, and carried me over the class, celebrating my birthday. The entire class sang Happy Birthday to the two of us (in English, of course). From this fifth grade class, there are still three people whom I talk to today, the rest I lost contact with.

School was one struggle, yet home was another

struggle, and even though for the first time in my life I did not have to work to survive, it was so difficult to adjust to this new life. I would go to school, where I could not communicate with people. I would come home to do homework; get some play time; see my older brother; and see my grandma, mom, little brother, and stepdad. Yet it felt like I was not at home. My home and life were back in Mexico, and although this seemed to be a *better* life, it was difficult. As Les Brown says, "Do what is easy and your life will be hard. Do what is hard and your life will become easy," and at this time, the easy thing was to go back to what I knew, what I was used to, speaking Spanish only, not being a kid, and working to survive. That was easy. Yet, as I recognized around that time, I was going through something hard since, in the end, my life would turn out to be easier—at least easier than it had been before.

Once I went from fifth to sixth grade, the school system put me into an ESL (English as a Second Language) classroom that was shared between fifth and sixth graders. This was the year that I actually started practicing and learning the English language. It was for sure simpler than fifth grade, as all of the students were bilingual and the majority of them did not speak or understand English and only spoke Spanish. From that perspective, I was in the right class and fit in perfectly. Also, since I had made friends in the fifth grade, I spoke to some of those students during sixth grade at recess, lunch, or after school.

As a matter of fact, I had my very first official girlfriend during this year. I was a kid with a label, yet this label felt special and good. I also got into some trouble several times during the year. The first time I got into a fight while going to school. The funny thing was that I became good friends with this person, and even now, we still talk. The second time, I almost did not graduate from elementary school because I always believe in defending others at any cost, and I would defend those who were being bullied and could not defend themselves.

This actually happened to my older brother while we were in Mexico, and I stood up to his bullies and got into a fight defending him. This was exactly what happened in fifth grade while a classmate was being bullied. Even though I did not know him, I stood up to defend him. He is still a good friend of mine. In the sixth grade, the same thing happened, and I got into a fight with another student, who was in the same grade. Given that it was so close to graduation, we were taken to the principal's office and told that we wouldn't graduate.

Thank God we were forgiven, and I was able to graduate (to this day, I do not believe my parents know about this particular elementary school fight). After only two years in the US elementary system, I still talk to four of the friends I made there and see them frequently.

Although I graduated, I was still having a difficult time fitting in and feeling at home. I remember one day when I was so upset, and as I was speaking to my dad, I told him that I did not want to be in the US and wanted to go back to Mexico to be with my grandma and have my old life back. My grandma had gone back to Mexico after a year in the states. I did not see her again for three years; she first came back in 1994 right before I graduated from middle school). I even told him that he was no one to me, and he could not tell me what to do.

As I reflect on that moment in my life, even though I was unhappy, I was wrong. My dad was not only supporting my mom and her two kids, he was also providing a chance at life for me, and I was not grateful enough. Nowadays, it is hard to find a man who will go above and beyond for someone like myself who isn't related to him through blood.

"If somebody offers you an amazing opportunity but you are not sure you can do it, say yes – then learn how to do it later."
—*Richard Branson*

A TRANSITION

I n mid-1992, I transitioned from elementary school to middle school, and many of the classmates I'd known from elementary ended up attending the same middle school. I did not feel too lonely after all, given that I had some old classmates (who, by this time, I considered friends) attending the same middle school. Even better, my older brother and I had at least one year together, so we would go to and leave school together, just like old times in Mexico. Having been in the US for two years, both my older brother and I were able not only to communicate with others in English, we had also learned how to speak it and write it. We were a bit beyond proficient, and that was a great accomplishment given that we'd only been here for such a short time.

A lesson to be learned from this is, no matter how hard things might seem, and no matter whether or not you are able to fit in, anything is possible. As long as you can accept and adjust with what emerges, life will turn out to be good.

One thing that perhaps was a bit different for us was the fact that in a city as big as Los Angeles, there were so many different cultures. With that, there was also conflict and, to an extent, racism. Racism was something that we did not really encounter in Mexico; at the end of the day, there was really only one race there. This was a challenge because there were so many adolescents who were involved in either gangs or tagging crews (which were, for the most part, segregated by race). It had an almost epidemic effect with so much negative influence, and although we stayed far away from it, it was hard not to stumble upon it.

One thing that I still cannot understand is that there were many students who had also migrated to the US—not just from Mexico and other parts of Latin America—and yet, instead of appreciating the opportunity, they fell into drugs, gangs, and tagging crews. Not only did they consciously make this choice, it seemed as though many of them were destined to come and waste their given potential in this land of opportunity. However, for my older brother and me, regardless of the bad influences, we had a different purpose. We did not allow these influences get the best of us, especially when we had accomplished what many had not in so many years, let alone during the two to three years we had in the states. We were able to communicate, defend, and speak our minds in the country's primary language.

I remember one day after school, my older brother and I had walked to the bus station to go home, and as we were waiting for the bus, a gang member (who looked as though he went to our middle school) came from behind and yanked off my older brother's gold necklace and my gold bracelet. As a matter of fact, I still have the scar in my right wrist to prove it. This is just an example of the adolescent corruption that was taking place around the schools, in the buses, while walking, etc., and at such an early age. I was only thirteen, and my brother was fifteen. It made one wonder if this truly was the land of opportunity, and if so, what was there to hope for in the future? Not only were the communities and cities dangerous, there was also the negativity, the negative influences, and the fact that, technically, we were not even legal residents. My future was unclear, and hope felt far from reach.

Nevertheless, neither my brother nor I gave in or gave up, and that is one of the most precious lessons you must learn, no matter where you are in your life at this moment. As Dale Carnegie said, "Most of the important things in the world have been accomplished by people who have kept on trying when there seemed to be no hope at all." As such, my older brother had much success in this school. I too had some great success for being in my first year of middle school. I was a great student and was liked by the teachers and faculty.

Speaking of great accomplishments, finishing the 1992-1993 school year had a major effect on me because I was losing my one true friend in life, my older brother. I lost him to what I now know was a great opportunity, yet at that time, I did not see it as such. My older brother was pretty smart, and he was able to excel in his academics. As a result, he was given a full-ride scholarship to one of the top high schools in the country, and shortly thereafter, moved to Minnesota. The hardest part was that the move was still too fresh for me; we'd only been in the US for three and a half years. I was still getting used to the life with my mom and stepdad, losing my older brother (not knowing when I would see him again), and also losing my grandma (who I'd grown up with, referring to her and knowing her as my mom). All I could think about was the feeling that I was in this country all by myself.

During the summer of 1993, I was given yet another challenge, and I called this a challenge because my mentor once told me that a challenge can be solved and is actually positive, whereas a problem implies a negative situation that is resistant to being fixed. The challenge I was facing was going to middle school with no older brother to talk to during or after school, and no grandma to call Mom.

Regardless of this emotional challenge, I was able to cope and stay focused on not fall into gangs, drugs, or negative influences. Eighth grade was a successful year. Not only did I receive over ten awards (for perfect attendance, scholastic achievement, and the like), I was also crowned the eighth grade prince. I'd work with no pay during my vacation in the school's cafeteria and also cleaned graffiti from the school's walls. On top of that, I graduated with honors and at the top of my class.

This was also the year when I met a girl who I spent much time with, and in fact, during this time it seemed as though the time we'd spend together would never end. One of my largest accomplishments was that I had the pleasure of being a speaker at my graduation, and the topic of my speech was "We choose our way."

You might wonder why this was such a big deal. For one, being an immigrant with no papers and only four years in the US (by the time I graduated from middle school), I had mastered English, I had my best year ever with straight As, I volunteered to help the community, and I was one of very few students from the entire eighth grade graduating class (over 200 students graduated) who received as many recognition awards as I did. I met a girl, and I finally felt like I was fitting into this new world.

"To be yourself in a world that is constantly trying to make you something else is the greatest accomplishment."
—*Ralph Waldo Emerson*

7

THE SPEECH

We Choose Our Way

Good morning, everyone! Today is a very especial day for all of us. We are the first eighth grade class graduating at Mt. Vernon Middle School. I feel so honored today to represent my friends and peers on this occasion.

First of all, I would like to say something to our faculty at Mt. Vernon. On behalf of the eighth-grade class, I would like to thank you for all the encouragement you have given us over the last two years.

Next, on behalf of the eighth grade, I would like to say something to our parents. You have always been there when we have needed you. You made sure that we got to school and got there on time. Also, you strongly encouraged us to do our homework when we didn't want to. This has given us a discipline that will help us in the future.

And finally, I will like to say something to the graduates today. We have been here at Mt. Vernon Middle School for two years, and it is now time to go on. We have finished our experience here, and it is now time to face new ones. Many of us are going to choose a way that would get us into college. We would choose a good education and a good life. Others, unfortunately, will choose the way of gangs and drugs. For them, the future looks dark. My challenge to all of us today is to choose the way of education. In this choice, we will not only improve our own lives, but we will also set an example for our community.

As I close, again I would like to say, we have much to be thankful for. We have many memories to take with us as we leave Mt. Vernon, and again on behalf of the eighth grade, I thank our principal, teachers, families, and honored guests for all they have done to help us see our dream come true.

8

GROWING UP

As I started my high school years, I was finally in a good place mentally. I had a girlfriend (who I'll refer to as Mona, which was the nickname given to her by mutual friends). I had many friends, I was nowhere near gangs or drugs, and I was a strong student taking advanced classes in my ninth grade year. The first year of high school, I joined the JV baseball team, kept up with my studies, and focused on moving forward and staying out of trouble.

Tenth grade, however, was a different story. I was always focused in my studies, except this year I was faced with a new challenge and a new temptation. Although I was solid in my academics, I was once told I lacked a father figure in my early years. I had built a good relationship with my stepdad, and as a matter of fact, I did not see him as my stepdad; I saw him as my dad. Yet not having my older brother, having a younger brother who was too small even to understand or talk to, not having my mom and dad around as often due to their work schedules, and never having a father figure as a kid might have led me to temptation.

In reality, I don't know if that's truly what contributed to my decisions. I do believe, however, that we can determine our fate and make our own choices.

During this school year, Mona got pregnant, and our biggest challenge was that we were kids having a kid. This by itself was very challenging because we needed to figure out how to continue to move forward. Even more importantly, we both had strong beliefs about life and against abortion. By the time we both felt it was time to speak to our parents, all I can remember is the fear we had. We faced my parents first and then her mom. (Her dad at that time did not like me and perhaps did not support me given that she was his only daughter; I likely would have felt the same way if I were in his shoes at that time).

My parents were absolutely disappointed, yet they were supportive and with us on this new journey. On the other hand, her mom's fear of what her husband would say caused her to react quickly, and the same day that we talked to her, she told my parents and me that she didn't want to deal with it, and Mona would have to leave and start her life with me.

At that time, we were both fifteen (she is six days younger than I am), and once again, just like in Mexico, I had to grow up fast. This time, it wasn't just for *me* to survive, it was also to provide for Mona and my child. One thing that we learned later, that helped us during high school, was that we were not the only teen couple having a child. There were other teen parents, and some of them were among our common friends. Growing up responsible, and knowing that I grew up with no real father as a kid, was what gave me the strength to overcome challenges I thought I would never face.

At this time we were both still kids, so we lived at my parents' house. They even gave up a room for us to live in as a couple. On top of that, I started helping my dad in the middle of the night delivering newspapers from the Los Angeles Times in areas such as Santa Monica and Marina Del Rey. This was difficult for me because I never gave up in school, so I had to go to school, work during the night with my dad, get little sleep, and then go back to school.

In the end, even with all those challenges, we were blessed with a total of three baby showers. As I finished the tenth grade, I had to change tracks from B track to C track. (We had three tracks, all based on students' concentration and academic achievements.) Mona and most of my friends were in B track. The reason I had to change was that the type of classes I had taken the previous years and the next high-level classes I had to take were only offered on C track. In order for me to continue to take higher-level classes, I needed to make the change, or I wouldn't have moved to the next level in my current track.

This was great news for me because I was expanding my scholastic knowledge. However, having a kid and being a family man was not easy at all. The first months of the eleventh grade school year were not as bad because the different tracks did not affect our lives. At least, not until later on, however the change ended up being positive, and we dealt with what emerged and made the best out of it.

I still remember the day before my beautiful daughter was born. Mona was not in school due to her pregnancy, and I was in class as if everything were okay. I remember both my parents standing outside my last classroom period, and all they said as soon as I came out was, "It's time." We immediately left the school and hurried to the hospital, as Mona had been admitted earlier that day (September 11).

I arrived at the hospital, and it was a long night. The following day, September 12, 1996, at 6:00am, my daughter was born. I was there for the entire delivery; it was a miracle of God. We named her Daisy Espino. Being the student that I was, I left the hospital to go to school. That day was tiring, as I had not slept much; during the night, I was working on my homework.

9

DRIVE AND DETERMINATION

Right after school that day, I hurried out, as I was excited to see my child, and yet I came across another challenge. This time, it was with Mona's mom and family. I was not allowed to see or take my daughter from their house. In the end, everything was worked out, and Mona, Daisy and I went back to my house.

Although it seemed as though I was prepared for this life, it hadn't sunk in how difficult it would be. As the days went by, it became harder and harder to see my future, growing up as a teenager raising a child and ensuring that my child would get a fair chance at life. As I thought of Muhammad Ali's words: "Children make you want to start life over," I said to myself and remember telling my child and Mona that I would do whatever it took to ensure that my daughter had a better life than I did. I made a promise to give her everything I did not have as a child—a life where she did not have to work to survive, options, and the opportunity to experience life from a different perspective and see it with different eyes than I had as a child. I knew that from that moment forward, I would have to work harder than ever.

So the questions were: How do I stay focused in school? How do I continue to concentrate on my studies? How do I raise a child? The answer, as I see it now, was: with much certainty and a clear focus. My drive during my last two years of high school was the fact that I had made a promise, and the only way to make sure I kept that promise was to keep up with my academics and make money. I also knew that as my daughter was growing, I did not want her to grow up with strangers. I wanted her to only grow up with people Mona and I knew we could trust.

One benefit that really helped us through our high school years was that, during eleventh grade, I changed tracks due to my academics, and Mona stayed in the same track. That meant that during the semester, Mona and I were only together in school for two months; the other four months were rotated between the two of us. This made it easier to take care of our daughter. For two months we had a family member taking care of her, the next two months Mona took care of her, and the final two months it was my turn. This gave us a pretty good routine, and it allowed us to manage tasks and priorities during each semester.

That year was challenging, as I had to be a father, which meant staying up late plenty of nights taking care of my daughter and/or working on school projects. I was fortunate to have my parents' support and assistance, especially during her first year. Even with the number of responsibilities I had, I always took care of my academics and involvement with school, and again won the title of eleventh grade prince for my class.

Just three months into the new school year, my parents had been working on legalizing my status in the US since I was still an illegal citizen and therefore could not officially work to take care of my family. To my surprise, the only way for me to get my legal status was for my stepdad to legally adopt me (he is a US Citizen), which meant that I had to take his last name. This was so hard for me. Although I was grateful to be able to work legally in the US while my permanent residence was being processed, I felt robbed of my identity. And, for the second time in my short life, I had changed last names.

My legal name changed from Cesar Espino Martinez (under Mexico laws) to Cesar Roman (under US laws). This legal name change forced me to switch homerooms in school, as homerooms were based on last-name lettering. I was so angry about the last name change, not recognizing that this gift given to me by my father would give me greater opportunities to grow and excel in this country. I went to the school and I did whatever I could to have my old and new last names combined through hyphenation. After a few months, I was able to make the change on school records, and from that point forward, at least on school paperwork, I was known as Cesar Roman-Espino.

One's name is so critical to his identity, and in just seventeen years I had gone through three. Not only did I get a number of questions from my classmates, I had to further explain the change and the reason behind it, then work to get everyone used to calling me by my new name while not forgetting that I was still an Espino.

"You have to know your identity. It's the biggest thing in wanting to pursue creative dreams."
—*Lauren Daigle*

My senior year was supposed to be the year that every high school student looks forward to, given the number of activities. It's a year to have fun and enjoy with friends, and the year when you want to solidify deep connections as you go to the next chapter of life, college. This was not to be my reality, as I had to really step up my game as a father, a family man, and a student. By this time, my daughter was already walking (she started walking at eleven months), and that meant she was curious about wandering everywhere.

I also came into the twelfth grade with all AP Classes (AP English, AP Calculus, AP History, and AP Physics), a new name I was just getting used to, a role as a committed father, and the ability to legally work. It would be a lie to say it was an easy year. I knew I had to work to support myself and my family, and as such, I had work experience for sixth period, which gave me the ability to work in school or actually take an offsite job and leave the school by the end of fifth period.

I was able to officially get my first job working for AMC Theaters at the Century City Mall, and I started as a part-time worker and an usher, primarily cleaning theaters and the floor, making only $4.25/hour. As the months went by, I was promoted to concession stand worker and was able to get more hours. When Mona was not in class, she was able to stay with our daughter, and when she was taking after-school classes and I was working, Daisy would stay with family members.

I still remember my high school years very clearly. I got up early to be at school by 7:30am. I got out of school after fifth period, took a forty-five minute bus ride to get to the theater, and started work at 3:00pm. I got off work at 11:00 or 11:30pm and took another forty-five minute bus ride back to my house. I did homework once I got home as well as on the bus, during my break, and whenever else I found time to do it. This was my daily routine, day-in and day-out, and it was hard.

By the end of my first semester as a senior, and for the

very first time in my years of schooling here in the US, I received a D in my AP English class. In order not to let it affect my GPA, I signed up to re-take an English class during my vacation to bring up my grade. Also, given my work and responsibility to my family, I had no choice but to drop all my AP classes. It was simply too much to manage. I did such a great job at AMC that within six months I was promoted, and then a few months later, I was made a lead.

Soon enough, my high school years were coming to an end, and during the second semester I started bringing my daughter around the school, especially when Mona was in school and I was on vacation yet still had to work at night. I specifically remember two instances that year. Once, I was taking the bus to drop off my daughter with Mona right after school, as I needed to go to work. As I took the bus ride, I talked with a few friends (if you could even call them friends) and the conversation was nothing but negative. One particular person laughed and straight out told me that I would never be anyone or anything, and that having a kid at an early age was a huge setback. A second instance was similar, except this person was actually my neighbor and a longtime friend. Not only did we hang out together (even with his entire family), we had taken trips together. He was a pretty negative, arrogant person, and his message was the same as my school friend's, yet a bit more direct. He said I was dumb, I had made a huge mistake, and I would never become anyone. Talk about encouragement! Yet these are two prime examples of why I am where I am, after all I've been through. I knew there was more for me to give and much more for me to prove, not to anyone in particular beyond myself. I needed to ensure that I took care of my family and those who did believe in me.

As you look at today's society, we are faced with so much negativity, and many times these toxic people are cohabiting in your day-to-day life. They're your so-called friends, your boyfriend or girlfriend, your family members. They are all around, except you have the power to choose to separate yourself from these toxic people, and I have. These two people who clearly told me I wouldn't become anyone were removed from my life, and last I checked, they are in a much worse scenario than I am.

"Someone's opinion of you does not have to become your reality."
—*Les Brown*

During the last semester, I saved enough money to be able to afford my very first car—a used 1989 Chevy Station Wagon that cost me $500. This was my ride for a good portion of my senior year, and to an extent, many friends liked the fact that I had a car. As old as the car was, there was a limited number of students who had a car; I guess working hard did pay off, as I was one of few. Regardless of the age of the car, it did the job; it took me from point A to point B, similar to life. As long as you know where you want to go and have determination, life will create the path for you to get there.

"Begin with the end in mind."
—*Stephen Covey*

As I ended my senior year, I was content with the outcome, even after the odds had seemed to be against me. As a responsible father and dedicated student with a full-time job, I still found time to take part in my senior class council. I graduated with honors and was ready to take the next step in my adult life. My high school degree reflected my newly hyphenated last name. I was able to honor my dad and keep one of the last names I was born with. Perhaps the only negative was that my older brother was not at my graduation (he hadn't been able to make it to my middle school graduation either). The only ones who made it were my parents, my younger brother, and my daughter. Still, it was great walking on stage when your friends, classmates, and the world in general said it couldn't be done. As I walked across the stage, I was sure that many thought I wouldn't get the grades or the honors I did.

10

NOT SETTLING FOR LESS

I mmediately after high school, with the beliefs passed on to me by my parents in terms of getting a good education, getting a good job, and taking care of my family, I knew I had to pursue a degree. I knew that I needed to continue my education, and although I was accepted to traditional four-year college, I decided to enroll at a trade school (ITT Tech) to study engineering.

This did not last too long. Although I was passionate about school and education, I had to decide between education and supporting my family, allowing Mona to continue her higher education while I took care of her and Daisy. My ITT Tech days only lasted for about six months, and soon after I left college to focus one hundred percent on working and giving Mona the opportunity to study first while I took care of the family.

Having made that adjustment, I continued to work during the night at AMC and in the morning helped to care for my daughter. I continued to excel my work for AMC, built a great reputation with upper management, and ultimately became a supervisor. The challenge was that even working full-time as a supervisor, I was still not making enough to really provide for my family. Mona, my daughter, and I were still living with my parents in a two-bedroom apartment. One of the rooms was for the three of us, while the other room was for my mom, dad, little brother, and grandma, as she would come to stay for long periods of time.

I believe that because of the teachings of my grandma and the fact that I started working at such an early age, I always looked for ways to excel in my professional life. After working at the theater for over two years, I had met many people at the mall and had made friends (not to mention, it felt like everyone from my high school came to work at this mall, so that allowed me to connect with even more people). As I got to know other people, I was told that the mall was hiring security guards, and in search for more money, I applied. Shortly thereafter, I was hired and transitioned out of the theatre to mall security, making $7.50/hour.

This was actually a pretty awesome turn of events because when I was a little boy living in Mexico, I would tell my mom and grandma that all I wanted to be when I grew up was a police officer. In my eyes, at the age of nineteen, this was the closest I would get to being any sort of law enforcer. I was a peace officer, enforcing the rules and laws of the mall, and I also had the pleasure of working with local police officers during the weekend as they brought high school students under their police explorer program.

I remember a time when we were called about a disturbance taking place at the theater (ironically, the one I worked at previously), and indeed, there was a huge group of people causing a number of disturbances. For the first time, I felt like an actual police officer, as we had to create a human chain (locking our arms) to prevent this group of people from leaving the theater. This did not go as planned, and the group of people (both males and females) rushed to fight with us. We were on the second floor, so we all tumbled down the stairs. The security at the scene (including myself) had to use force to physically arrest this group of people with handcuffs while the actual police arrived to take them to the station.

This was an amazing experience, like another dream come true. The lesson to be learned here is that no matter how easy something might seem, at the end of the day, any harm or evil done to others will come back to hunt you and destroy you. These people were disturbing others, being loud, and felt they could do whatever they wanted. In the end, they were all arrested for breaking the law.

Always looking to grow and seeking that next opportunity, I needed to make more than I was as a mall security officer. One thing that stood out to me was seeing older people, from their mid-twenties to their early fifties, working at the same companies that I'd worked for. I said to myself, "That cannot be me in the future." I knew I had greater potential, and I couldn't be as complacent as these co-workers who felt it was okay to work at these jobs making next to nothing. I knew this was not for me, so I kept looking for that next opportunity. I learned that Express was looking for stockroom workers, and so I applied. This position paid a lot more than a security guard, and after my interview and first behavioral test ever, I was hired by Express at $9.00/hour (more than a 200% increase over my very first job at AMC, and in just four years).

Not only did I make a change in my job, I knew I had to go back to school if I wanted to continue to expand my professional career. As I looked at the different industries, I was looking for a profession in which I could have rapid career growth, a school that would allow me to get my degree quickly, and a school that could also give me enough flexibility to still have the full-time job I needed to support my family.

With these requirements, traditional school was out of the question, so I started to look at private schools. Knowing that there was a high demand on the technical side, with technology and computers being the next big thing, I found a private trade school. I enrolled at CLC (Computer Learning Center) to pursue my associate's degree.

Going back to school reminded me of my high school years, as I went to school Monday to Friday from 8:00am until about 2:30pm, and I worked during the evenings. This time, the education was not free, and I had to get student loans to pay for it, which meant that there were higher stakes and I could not let any of it go to waste or I'd be throwing money away. Attending and being part of this school provided me with two other experiences that I still think of and apply in many situations in my life.

First, there was a diversity of people, not only from different ethnicities but also from different age groups. The first thing I realized was that if you badly want something, you are never too old to go out and get it. Regardless of your age or background, you have the ability to reach your goals. When I learned this at just nineteen, it opened my eyes because there were so many people who already had jobs, yet they also had a drive or a particular motivation to keep learning and expanding their knowledge and were back in school for growth. Education is powerful.

The second realization was that every single student in the school had a monetary obligation to learning and graduating, but still treated the experience as though it were high school or an otherwise free education. Even if the students themselves did not take out a loan, their parent(s) or another family member(s) were carrying the burden of their student loan. There were students who were just wasting their time, still trying to figure it out, letting time just pass by as if it wasn't important. I tend to refer to this group of people as seat warmers, because that is the only real action they are taking. It baffled me to see students take this experience for granted, yet this can be seen every day in schools, at work, and in neighborhoods—people look at time as if it isn't important, as if you have all the time in the world. And then they realize on their death bed or last days of life that it is too late to leave a legacy, leave a purpose, and get back time.

Similarly, there are many people (the majority of the population, it seems) who accept what is given to them, making no effort to make their lives any better by trying to figure things out. They let the days come and go with no drive to take action or make changes. People are just floating through and "getting by," being a seat warmer for their entire life. I encourage you to take these lessons and not stay stagnant, not be complacent, not let yourself down, and know that there is a bigger plan for your existence in this world. Allow that purpose to flourish and be manifested through your life.

Up to this point, I learned several lessons, and a common denominator between all them was that you *can* dictate, manage, and control your life. No matter when the world, society, or your circle of friends tells you no, puts obstacles in front of you, or throws curve balls at you, your fight and dedication can overcome anything. You have the answers to turn every negative obstacle, every no, into a certain and positive yes.

After studying others who came from other places in

the world, specifically Latin America, I've realized that many of them gave up too soon. Many of them took for granted this opportunity. I am not saying that by this time I was on top of the world, however I know for a fact that while it took me two years to learn English, it took others much longer. I am saying that some decided to take the path of gangs only to fit into a different society and disregard education, while I fought that same temptation, regardless of the fact that I had no one. I choose to fight those influences and instead further my education. When others did not have to worry about having their identity changed time and time again, I eventually embraced it, dealt with what emerged, and used that to keep me going.

These are choices that we all have, and the influences of others should not dictate your future but instead only serve as guidance. In the end, the ultimate decisions are made by the person you see each and every day in the mirror when you wake up. One way to summarize the fact that the decision and the control is on your hands was best said by Hal Elrod: "It is often said that everything happens for a reason, but you must embrace the perspective that it's never a reason that is predetermined or out of your control." The excuse made by playing the blame game— that everything happens for a reason—is not entirely true. You still have a choice and have control of the situation, so take control of your life.

In 1999, after several years, I was once again reunited with my older brother when he relocated back to Los Angeles. By this time, there had been a few changes in both of our lives; things were not the same.

First, we were both grown men, and we both had the drive to become more than we could imagine. Second, I had a family. Not only did I have a girlfriend, I also had a child. My brother also had a girlfriend, who I was able to meet for the first time. We were reunited at a point when we had different life paths, and interestingly, my grandma always pictured us together for the rest of our lives. If you recall, my grandma had asked the city officials to allow her to build a house, and in this house, she built two rooms that were exactly the same size with a door in the middle to allow us to go back and forth. My grandma was raised believing that we would always be together, and her thought process was to build those two rooms where my older brother and I would grow and create our own families, each living in one of the rooms with our kids and our wife. However, our destinies had taken us down different paths and toward different lives.

The good thing was that regardless of where we ended up, we were back together, and we still had a great future ahead of us because we both grew up knowing to never give up and to work hard to reach the top.

PART III

EARLY ADULTHOOD

11

FINDING MY WAY

The next major phase of my life was my twenties, and perhaps these are the years during which it's most critical for people to stay focused, yet ninety-five percent of people take these years for granted. I, on the other hand, had no choice, and I was glad for that, as it kept me moving forward and pushing hard to provide for my family.

By the age of twenty, I was going to school and working full-time. During this time, it felt overwhelming, yet I did not give in, I did not give up, I continued to look forward, and I continued to work hard to reach my education goals. Given my dedication to a higher education, I received my associates degree in Computer Systems and Networking Technology and graduated Summa Cum Laude in September 2010. I was also inducted into the National Vocational Technical Honor Society (NVTHS) for outstanding career and technical achievement. By the time I finished my associates degree and sought opportunities with computer and tech companies like IBM, I'd decided to attend a trade school to receive some certifications.

The trade school I attended had classes around Microsoft products, Novell, and CompTIA. Looking to expand my hardware and software skills, I received my credentials in December 2010. I received the A+ certification from CompTIA and Microsoft Products related to MCP (Microsoft Professional), MCP+I (Microsoft Professional + Internet), and MCSE (Microsoft Professional Systems Engineer).

Having so much dedication to my studies, being persistent and hardworking, having an associate's degree, and gaining these four certifications made me feel unstoppable. I believed that I could go to any company and make better money than I was making at Express. Not only was I in debt by $35,000 between my associates degree and my trade certifications, I was not able to find a job in a credible company. Although I had all this educational training, I had no real work experience. No company would take me at an entry level without any work experience, and the only way to get into any of these companies was through someone I knew who already worked at one of them. Unfortunately, I did not have any connections, nor did I have a network of IT professionals.

The one thing that kept me going was that I never gave up, and I continued to work at the retail store while at the same time working from home on computer hardware and software by building towers from the ground up. Even when the professional world of IT industry said no, I continue to move forward.

"The only thing a person can ever really do is keep moving forward. Take that big leap forward without hesitation,

> without once looking back. Simply forget the past and
> forge toward the future."
> ——*Alyson Noel*

As I entered 2001, I was excited to be planning my first international trip (besides traveling back and forth many times to Mexico as a teenager), this time I was going to El Salvador. This was exciting, yet a bit scary since it was the first time Mona and I were taking our daughter—who was just four years old—out of the country, let alone to a third-world country. The reason why we decided to go to El Salvador was that Mona was born there, and we went to visit her family. El Salvador is, in many way, similar to my birth country, except that it seems to have greater corruption, a less supportive government system for its citizens, and a greater amount of poverty.

I remember one of our first days there. I had gone out to make a call at a public phone with Mona's cousin, and while he was making the call, I was randomly approached by a gang member from the Mara Salvatrucha (also known as MS-13), who tried to rob me. It was a good thing Mona's cousin knew him from somewhere, and he left me alone. MS-13 has become an international criminal gang that originated in Los Angeles, CA between the 1970s and the 1980s, formed by undocumented immigrants. Today, this gang is all over the US, Canada, Mexico, and Central America, and the members are mostly of Central American descent with the majority being from El Salvador. This was the only bad experience I had with a local. Besides that, the trip was good. That is, until a day before our departure back to the US.

On Saturday, January 13, 2001, Mona and I were at the *mercado* (market) in Santa Ana purchasing stuff to bring back with us to the states. At approximately 9:33am PST, there was a major earthquake. The magnitude of it was 7.6, and mind you, the *mercado* we were in was made similarly to many of the homes, primarily out of sheet metal and plywood. The earthquake shook the entire *mercado* so hard that everything was falling down, hitting people and creating major chaos both inside and outside. At that particular moment, I was more worried about my daughter, as she had stayed behind with Mona's family in the house. It took us about sixty minutes to get out of the *mercado* and another twenty minutes to get to the house.

Upon our arrival at the house, my first worry was whether my daughter was safe, and indeed she was, although she was a bit frightened. This earthquake was the strongest magnitude in the country since 1950. As a result, there was major damage to the entire country, including the international airport. Because of its damage, flights were cancelled and we were forced to stay another week in El Salvador.

As a young father, I had to find a way to explain to my four-year-old what was happening and continue to comfort her during this difficult time. The best thing I could come up with was telling my daughter that the neighbor was playing his music loud and the earth was dancing to the rhythm. As funny as it may sound, it worked, and it kept my daughter at peace. Mona, not so much. She was terrified, and each time the earth shook, my daughter would say that the neighbor was playing the music out loud.

Since this earthquake, El Salvador experienced more than 2,500 aftershocks, some measuring a magnitude as high as 5.5. It began to feel as though it was normal for people to be sleeping outside; you just never knew when there was going to be another aftershock. Our primary objective was to leave El Salvador and head back out to the states. We were pushing on our side to get the next flight out, and at the same time, my parents were pushing on their side (in the US) to get us a flight out. Finally, a week later, I was able to secure a flight out, and we gladly left. Talk about an experience, my first official international trip (outside of Mexico) with our daughter, and to our surprise, we got hit with the largest earthquake in El Salvador's history! Thank God we were not injured, and we survive this catastrophe. As of today, an estimated 944 casualties and 5,565 injuries from this massive earthquake have been reported.

Never having been out of the country, I was glad to be home, and by this time, I recognized the US as my home. Also by this time, I had my US resident status, and I was just waiting to complete the mandatory time required by the USCIS (U.S. Citizenship and Immigrations Services) to submit my application for citizenship. On top of experiencing one of the largest earthquakes in my life during this year (second to my first experience, the 1985 Mexico earthquake, which had a magnitude of 8.0), I was officially twenty-one, and this was the beginning of a new chapter. From society's perspective, I was an adult, although in reality, I'd been grown up since the first day I started working while in Mexico, and certainly since I had the responsibility of raising another human being.

12

GAINING STABILITY

This was the year I sought greater stability in my professional career. Without knowing it beforehand, Mona had a distant relative who worked at a computer shop, and through his connections I was able to get a job as a computer technician. I finally had the opportunity to put into practice the theory and teachings I'd studied. I had changed my schedule at Express to only work mornings and worked in the afternoons at the computer shop. As Mark Zuckerberg pointed out, "In a world that's changing really quickly, the only strategy that is guaranteed to fail is not taking risks." For the first time, I took a risk. Although small, it was still a risk because I was making the transition to leave a job that did not require any special skills, training, or knowledge (retail) to one that required that I knew what I was doing, applying both technical skills and logistical thinking to get the job done.

As I continued to work at the computer shop, that role was definitely a different type of challenge. Shortly thereafter, I was given the opportunity to go out in the field and go to people's houses to troubleshoot and fix their computer issues. It was scary but rewarding at the same time. I also started troubleshooting computer issues at my house as a side hobby, with the intention of further understanding the ins and outs of a computer. As I got more comfortable, I made a complete transition out of the retail world and into a full-time computer technician role. This was an exciting time for me, as I finally got into a field that related to my associate's degree and trade schooling. I also decided to start going to computer fairs to get further involved in this field, which led to some wonderful opportunities down the line.

Around this time, I began experiencing difficulties in my personal relationship with Mona, something I did not think would ever happen. I thought this would be the only relationship I would ever have. We had difficult times, and we were working through those challenges. As we continued our relationship, I continued to evaluate my professional career. Looking at the computer shop, I noticed that while it was a good start, it was not a large enough company to leverage my skills toward a successful future. The computer shop provided a great opportunity to get my feet wet, but it would not allow me to grow. I still wanted to work for a larger company such as IBM, so I networked further and began to search for openings at a larger corporation.

I came across a temporary agency that focused solely on people with an IT background, and by working through them I was able to land several temporary jobs that gave me more exposure in this industry. (I did this while still working at the computer shop.)

Several months later, the temporary agency was able to position me on what seemed to be a steady project, and I was asked to work at a logistics company in their IT department as help desk and user support. Given such an opportunity and the time requirement for this job, I decided to leave the computer shop. Professional life was good and my career was finally taking a good direction, but my personal life was still struggling. Then, just when things were going great for the first time, I was laid off from my job. The company that hired my temporary services had to make some financial cuts, and given that I only had worked for them for two months, it was easy for them to end my assignment. For the first time, I was out of a job and had nothing to fall back on.

I continued to work with the temporary agency, and they were able to give me one- or two-day assignments as well as some week-long temporary jobs, but nothing concrete. I hoped that something great would come, and I'm glad I did not let fear get the best of me. After about a month without a job, the company that laid me off contacted my temporary agency and specifically asked for me to return to work with them in the IT department. This was fantastic. At the end of the day, I did what I've always believed—always do your best at any given job (and I gave it my best even when, at first, it was only for two months). You just never know when you will be needed, and it's very important never to burn any bridges and always give it your best.

As we entered 2002, the logistics company was very pleased with my work ethic and requested to hire me as a full-time employee. In just a few months working as a temporary employee, I focused on my job, I proved myself, and once again my professional life continued to grow. Given how busy I was with work and my personal life, I had lost contact with many of my high school friends. The reality is that when you are in high school and know so many people, you never think about losing contact. You assume you will always have those friends next to you, but that's not entirely true. Some friends will stick with you, and many will fall off. We do not understand this concept while we're in school, however after high school, many take a different journey because of family, careers, disciplines, values, and principles. No one really knows the path one will take, and life tends to get in between relationships.

By April 2002, I'd begun my next chapter in life with a full-time position in a national logistics company, doing what I liked. Life was great, and a side business I had started in 2001 began to grow for me as well. I had begun C.E. Computers as my side business, and I focused on building relationships with friends, co-workers, friends of my parents, and friends of friends. Because I loved building computers and had gone to many computer fairs, I started building computers from scratch for other people. I extended my services by offering computer support and repair by appointment only. I worked out of my living room and eventually had computers parts on hand to help me be more effective when repairing and/or selling parts.

My life was being defined and I had a great job; a good side business; a loving grandma; parents; a younger and an older brother; a beautiful, healthy, and educated daughter; and life was good. Except, I had a broken relationship. It was difficult to understand how I could have just about everything yet still be missing something. Perhaps it was the absence of a father figure when I was a kid, perhaps it was the fact I grew up too fast, perhaps it was my drive for greater achievement, but at that time I didn't know what it was. I just know that I did not stop running. I had faced many challenges, taken some risks, made several mistakes, and excelled in many areas, and yet never could I have imagined putting myself through the following experience.

13

A DETOUR

I struggled with a short fuse, was having difficulties in my relationship with Mona, and just two weeks before my next trip to Mexico (when my parents were to renew their marriage vows at my dad's home town) I had a confrontation with Mona. July 14, 2002 suddenly became my largest challenge in life, as I was arrested and spent four days in jail. Thank God I was released with no charges, yet with a life-changing experience and lesson. I was released one day prior to leaving for Mexico.

Because we were celebrating my parents renewing their vows, my entire family attended the event. From my own family, there was myself with Mona and our daughter, except Mona just came for the party and returned back to the US on her own. I stayed behind with our daughter and the entire family. This was the day that my relationship with Mona came to an end. One of many lessons from this experience came to me by recognizing that I have to own my actions and work hard to gain the respect of others.

"He who is untrue to his own cause cannot command the respect of others."
—*Albert Einstein*

Once I dropped Mona at the airport, my older brother and his now-wife, my daughter, and I spent one week in Acapulco. My parents spent a few days with us and then returned to my dad's home town. Spending time with my family was great, yet seeing my daughter having so much fun was even greater. This gave me a new purpose in life. Aside from the promises I had made to my daughter when she was born; I knew I had to make another promise. Understanding that Mona and I would most likely end our relationship, I could not allow my daughter to grow up without a father figure the way I did, and I told myself that regardless of whether Mona and I ended, I would always be there for my daughter and would not allow our separation to come between us. While on vacation, I decided not to think or talk about the situation, only to enjoy each and every minute with my family, see my daughter smile, and give her all I could while we were in Acapulco. I would worry about what my life would be like after I returned to the US.

After spending a week on vacation, I came back to face reality and deal with the next steps of my life. After seven years of a relationship with Mona (of that, five years living together), we decided to part ways, and our relationship came to an end. Understanding that there was a child in the middle, we came to a mutual agreement to alternate weekends spent with our daughter. We also agreed to a monetary support arrangement to ensure that our daughter was taken care of. Mona moved out to an apartment with my daughter, and I stayed behind with my parents.

It's hard to understand why many couples who end up breaking up and have a kid (or kids) in the middle cannot work through their differences. Looking back at this lesson should help those struggling in their relationships to understand that the person who matters is not you, it's your child (or children). People waste so much energy fighting over insignificant things (money and materialistic items), not realizing that during these hard times, what is important is to become better people and work together for the best interest of the children. Working together as friends provides for a more promising future for the kids, and it also creates a more promising future for the adults, as there are no worries, no fights, and no stress.

I am so happy to know that any differences between Mona and me were left behind or put to the side; our main interest was ensuring that our daughter always had a mom and a dad, even if we were not all under the same roof. We also had such a great agreement that there was no need to get courts, lawyers, or anyone else looking at our business. Rather than waste money by paying others, we kept more money to take care of our daughter.

People tend to have higher pride and not see the harm that can be done to one's self and the children. I highly recommend that if you are going through something similar, work through your differences together to provide a better future for everyone involved. I also suggest not making the same mistake many people do, which is staying together in a non-working relationship because of kids. This is by far the largest mistake anyone can make. Using kids as the excuse to stay in a relationship that is going nowhere will only bring more harm, pain, stress, and unhappiness. Do not confuse the situation. If the differences cannot be worked on as couple, separating and working together to provide a better future together for your kids is the best decision one can make. Do not let the fear of not being with someone dictate your next steps or make you do things you will later regret.

"Sometimes good things fall apart so better things can fall together."
—*Marilyn Monroe*

From that point forward, my focus was working on my side business, working at my full-time job, and dealing with the new life I had—the single life. After just a few months working in the IT department for the logistics company, I'd built good working relationships with the regional director. Proving myself while working for this company provided me with another career opportunity.

I was approached by the regional director, who asked me if I wanted to transition out of the IT department and work in operations as one of the supervisors. Given the opportunity and my vision of working in the IT field managing other people, I decided this would be a good way for me to get experience in managing people and leading a team. This was the beginning of my management career, and I was responsible for leading a group of people to reach the company's goals and purpose.

Given this opportunity, and knowing that ultimately I would go back to the IT field, I decided to go back to school and enrolled in a bachelor's degree program for information technology. My thought process was that by getting the professional experience leading and managing people and by going back to school and further expanding my IT education, once I graduated I would be able to land a managerial position for a tech or IT company doing what I'd studied and loved, while at the same time have a higher leadership position.

It was a challenge to balance school, work, my daughter, and dating. As I continued to work for the logistics company, I had the pleasure of proving myself to my superiors, and I was rewarded with an opportunity to travel nationally, helping other locations and getting further leadership training. I was blessed to have the opportunity to travel and have the company take care of all my expenses. It was truly nice to know that an immigrant who worked as a kid to survive was now experiencing what many people only dream about. Truly, one can have and get anything they want by working hard, bringing value, and not building walls between yourself and what's possible for you.

14

SECOND ROCK BOTTOM

Success was just around the corner. In mid-2003 I graduated and received my bachelor's degree in Information Technology. Additionally, I had a good career, and even with my BSIT, I loved working with people so much that I ended up staying in operations. From that point forward, I didn't pursue a further career change. Besides, I was still missing the one thing that kept me from getting a job in this field to begin with: consistent experience working in the field. Although I felt more confident that I could get a job in the field even with my limited work experience, my two degrees, and my certifications, I would essentially start in a new company at an entry level, which meant I would take a pay decrease. Because I enjoyed what I was doing, I was not willing to take a pay reduction.

By this time, I was responsible for over eighty associates, had taken part in continuous improvement groups, had created processes that were deployed over multiple locations across the nation, and had traveled all over the place with the company. Work life was good, educational background was good as well. My one and only challenge was in the relationship arena.

Talking about relationships, and not necessarily knowing how to be single since I never had the opportunity to date or test the waters in my teens or young adult years, I got emotionally attached to a girl who ended up becoming my wife and turned out to be my next largest challenge and nightmare. I dated her for several months before we decided to get married, and as quickly as we got married, we ended the relationship and got divorced. Never did I imagine I would have another failed relationship, let alone a failed marriage. My mentor once told me that having a bad meal does not mean you stop eating; it only means you won't have that specific meal again. This is also true when it comes to a long-term relationship. Just because one fails at it once does not mean one cannot do it again, and again, and again until he finds true happiness.

However, the failed marriage was not the terrible experience. That was actually nothing compared to what it was about to happen.

I still remember it as if it were yesterday. It was a Friday afternoon in May 2004 , and I had my daughter for the weekend. I had moved out of my parents' house and was living in a two-bedroom apartment with my wife at the time (soon-to-be ex-wife). On this day, I was spending time with my daughter, watching a movie in the living room, and my then-wife was not content that my daughter was getting all the attention. Having learned from past experience, I offered for her to sit down next to us and watch a movie. After hearing her getting upset and start talking nonsense, I decided to go outside the apartment to take a breather. My mistake was going out and leaving my daughter behind to watch the movie, because the unexpected happened.

Out of anger, because I ignored her while she was arguing, my wife decided to lock herself inside the apartment while my daughter was still inside the house. I was so upset, and I demanded that she open the door. I was even more frightened because my daughter was inside and did not know what my wife would do to her (after all, her anger was due to my daughter getting all the attention). Not knowing what to do, I placed a call into 911. I was able to speak to the operator and explain the situation. I was told that they would see what they could do, but nothing was guaranteed. Shortly thereafter, my wife came out, looked at me, and said, "You are going to remember this, you will see." She kept walking and left. Of course, I only wanted to ensure that my daughter was fine, and she was.

Something deep down told me that it wasn't going to be a great weekend, and my gut told me to make some calls. I called Mona and explained to her what had happened, apologized to her, and asked her if she could pick up our daughter. I did not want her to see my wife and me fighting. I then made a second call to my best friend and told him I needed him to be there as my witness, given that I had a bad feeling. Thirty to forty-five minutes after my call, both Mona and my best friend showed up at my apartment. After another thirty to forty-five minutes, the sheriffs suddenly showed up, and the only thing going through my mind was that they finally showed up after I had called previously.

As the sheriffs approached my apartment, they asked if I was Cesar Espino, and I confirmed. Then my second rock bottom came unexpectedly. I thought they were there because of the 911 call I had made, but they'd actually come to arrest me.

My heart broke and I dropped to the ground. It was so hard to see my daughter watch the sheriffs placed the handcuffs on me. It was so hard to be taken away right in front of her. I explained to the sheriffs that I had done nothing wrong. I told them that my ex-girlfriend (Mona) and best friend were there to be my witnesses, and prior to that, my daughter could testify that I had not done anything to my wife. The sheriffs mentioned that my daughter was just a kid and her word would not suffice, especially when my wife had shown the authorities what she claimed to be domestic violence bruises. I suddenly knew what she meant when she told me I would remember that day.

I'm not sure which was more painful, being arrested for the second time and spending days in jail or having my daughter witness her dad being taken away. As I spent time in jail, I was worried about what to tell my employer, how I could fast-track my divorce, and what I could do to regain my integrity and life. Not knowing the degree of the bruises my wife had self-inflicted also worried me, because I thought my world could easily be over. I had the opportunity to speak to a district attorney and once again stated my case. I not only did not admit to something I did not do, I pleaded to be seen by a judge so I could find a way to be released. After staying positive, praying, and knowing deep down that I did not do anything wrong, I was released with no charges and no record whatsoever. The day I was released, my older brother and wife were waiting for me outside the jail. It seemed that they were in constant communication with the court, as they knew when I was going to get released. I was so happy to see them and be free once again.

We immediately went to my apartment to pick up some clothes. I had decided that I would file for divorce and move back in with my parents. To my surprise, my apartment was literally upside down, trashed, and many of my papers and pictures were all over the apartment as if a tornado passed through. The building's trash bin was filled with many torn pictures, papers, and personal items. My older brother and I had to go into the trash bin and dig out as many of my items as possible. This definitely gave me more reason to file for a divorce, and I did so immediately. The sad part is that it took me more time to get divorced than it took me to have an okay marriage. My wife clearly was looking to destroy my life, yet I did not let the circumstance get the best out of me. Life is full of punches and surprises, and it is up to us to take full responsibility of each situation, create our own path, and never give up, regardless of what happens along the way.

Nothing comes easy in this life, and to have a fulfilling life, a successful life, and a purposeful life you *must not allow anyone or anything* to tell you that you cannot overcome any obstacle. You can, you will, and you must.

The best choice I had was to move back with my parents while I got officially divorced, and approximately six months later, I was once again single. Because I had moved into my own place, I had purchased all the essentials for my apartment, and since I gave up my apartment and moved back to my parents' house, I had to fill my parents' apartment with all my belongings (they had no garage, and I did not have the money to spend on a storage unit). Although I moved back to my parents' house by myself, I had already experienced being on my own (even if it was for just a month or so), and my parents' apartment was not big enough for me *and* all my stuff. I decided to move out again, however I felt it was time to buy my own house. I had a good job to back me up, and felt I was responsible enough to take on my own place.

I was connected to a realtor who assisted me in finding my first house not too far from my parents. We initiated the process, and I provided all the necessary documents to purchase my very own home. I was so excited for this next stage in my life. I was able to secure a bank loan to fund my house, and expected to close on my home by the end of December.

Once again, life put a roadblock in front of me. The world was again telling me no, and fear returned. The company that I worked for laid me off just before I was given the keys to my home. It was devastating. I had endured so much to that point, and just when I was getting back on my feet again, I found myself unemployed, but this did not stop me. I did not allow the fear and this circumstance to change my plans, regardless of knowing that it wasn't going to be easy. I continued on, and just a month before my twenty-fifth birthday, I became a proud homeowner.

"Every problem is a gift–without problems we would not grow."
——*Tony Robbins*

"Remember, always give your best. Never get discouraged. Never be petty. Always remember, others may hate you. But those who hate you don't win unless you hate them. And then you destroy yourself."
——*Richard M. Nixon*

15

INVESTING IN MY FUTURE

The beginning of 2005 was challenging. I had no job, I had a mortgage payment, and I didn't know how to start all over again. Luckily, because my home closed escrow toward the end of the year, I had a few weeks to strategize and find a way to get back on my feet. It was hard, but when you fall, you have the choice to stay down or get up, and I chose to get up.

I attended several job fairs and gave my resume to everyone I came into contact with. I put up my resume on all the job sites and applied for multiple positions. I was contacted by a temporary agency, and at that time, any job was better than no job. I needed to bring in money, and I was not about to let go of what I had worked so hard for.

While doing temporary work, I was placed at a dairy logistics company in the City of Industry (which was a good hour or so away in LA traffic). It wasn't ideal, but it was a job. After a month as a temporary employee, I was hired on as a direct employee. Once again, I had to prove myself and show this company that I was more than capable of getting the job done. I was moved around to cover multiple shifts, and the worst shift for me was the graveyard shift. I did this for about four months until I was able to return to the morning shift.

This was also the year when I officially became a US citizen, which was not an easy thing to accomplish because although I had no criminal record, I had to still provide a full report of both of my previous arrests per USCIS regulations. This process took much longer than expected, and I had started it two years prior. As soon as I had my citizenship interview, I was able to provide all the information required regarding my non-criminal record, prove that Mona and I had an agreement for taking care of our daughter without having to worry about any child services, and prove I was worthy of being part of this awesome country.

This was also my opportunity to regain part of my identity. A beautiful thing about becoming a US citizen is that during the process you have the opportunity to make a change to your name, and I took that opportunity. I wanted to honor my dad for being a true father even though he did not create me, and for always being there for me and my entire family. He is an honorable man who assisted me in opening up the doors to excel in this country. Keeping that in mind, I change my name from Cesar Roman to Cesar Roman Espino. I made Roman my middle name and put back Espino as my primary last name. I did not keep my second last name of Martinez, at least not on any legal paperwork.

My mid-twenties were awesome. There were so many positive challenges and so many great outcomes; I could not have asked for more. I felt like I was on top of my life, moving forward, and investing in my future.

I was found on jobsinlogistics.com by an international freight forwarder located just a few minutes from LAX.

One of the things I clearly remember from my interview is that although I had a Bachelor's Degree in IT, my interviewer (who turned out to be my boss later on) mentioned that he appreciated and recognized that getting a degree was not an easy thing. He went on to say that he really appreciated my dedication, and that it spoke highly of my character. Even if the available position was not related to my degree of study, he mentioned that he had looked at my resume from a year prior and was waiting for budgets to open up so he could interview me. The interview and the words mentioned were all positive, and it made me realize that even if you do not get into your field of study, the discipline, dedication, and commitment you invest in getting through something has a larger reward, and it certainly showed up for me through this opportunity.

After a year at the dairy company, I was extended a really good offer making more money than I ever had in my first managerial position for any company. I jumped on the opportunity for several reasons. One, this company was global, and I could see how I could expand in this industry. Two, I was given a managerial position, something I'd never before had. Three, it was just thirty minutes from my new home. And four, the pay was great. After a year of struggle, 2006 looked very promising and things were falling back into place. Sometimes not expecting anything will return a greater result, so always be prepared to take on any great opportunity.

"Expect the best. Prepare for the worst. Capitalize on what comes."
—*Zig Ziglar*

In my personal life, things were going well. At just twenty-six years old, I felt I could do more and take additional risk to grow. Right before I switched companies, I decided to invest, and my investing career continued as I acquired my second SFR (single family residence). At that time, I was not working with anyone; I was doing all my investments on my own. My primary home had increased in value, and I leveraged the equity on that home, refinanced, and took out some money to purchase my second home and pay off my vehicle. As soon as I acquired this new home, I began working to get someone to rent the house, and before I knew it, I was a landlord.

Working for this international company was new for me, and I am glad that my direct manager believed in me and gave me all his support. Just a few months into this new job, I had positioned myself in a space where I found myself making positive changes that impacted the company and created more business opportunities. I was challenged in learning international business as it dealt with air, ocean, and domestic transportation and also learning how to grow the warehousing department. From a business perspective, I was able to get involved with the departmental financials and start to understand more in detail the Profit and Loss statements and plan for growth as well as build relationships with vendors and customers.

After I showed my boss my interest in expanding the warehousing business, he sent me on my very first international business trip to learn as much as possible from one of the sister companies that had already created a complete WMS (Warehouse Management System) and a warehouse operation. My objective was to learn as much as possible and gain enough knowledge to implement the same system at my current location. I was so excited to finally travel internationally on business that I immediately worked on getting my first official US passport.

I also joined a partnership and opened up my first janitorial company, rendering cleaning services to businesses and restaurants. This business venture was new, and I was relying on my business partner to help us grow and expand. I took care of the financials (acting as CFO) and he looked over the sales and operations (acting as COO). Looking back, not only was I a homeowner, a landlord, working full time for an international company, a new US citizen, and now a small business owner, I was also still in my mid-twenties. All those hard moments, the things I'd gone through, and the things I overcame were well worth it. I can relate to what Walt Disney said: "We keep moving forward, opening new doors, and doing new things because we're curious and curiosity keeps leading us down new paths." Life has the ability to create, outline, and provide multiple paths of wealth. You simply must never give up.

As the months went by, it appeared that things were getting better and better, and 2017 brought about another phase in my life where I began to like the idea of international travel, for both business and pleasure. I made several personal trips to El Salvador after I reconnected with an old friend. This time, I experienced the country a bit more freely, renting a car and moving from town to town as if it were my own. After several trips, I came to know many places. I've traveled several times to Mexico, to several different states in the US with my daughter, and to three countries outside the US. More importantly, I've kept my promise to ensure that my daughter had all the things I did not have as a kid: a father figure, toys, travel, a better life, and not having to worry about working. Life as I knew it was great. I was more than grateful for all of the doors that had opened, and I was glad that, even with fear, I pushed through and moved forward when those doors did open.

Speaking of opportunities and doors opening, I made my third investment and acquired my third house. Not only was this a good investment in terms of building my rental portfolio but I was also looking at a career change. My former boss (the one who hired me at the international company) contacted me, as he had left the company a few months prior to work for another international forwarder. He wanted to see if I had any interest in following him and being the primary manager of a new location they were looking to open. This was a no-brainer for me. Not only did I get to make a career move but I was also given the opportunity to operate my own building, and even better, it was going to be built from the ground up. I would be the key person in charge of this location. This gave me the ability to expand and grow as a manager, manage company financials for this location with full responsibility for P&L, recruit and mentor my own team of people, and build a working relationship with new customers and a few old customers relocating to this location. The first months were challenging, but the type of challenge that is good because I was full of excitement in growing this business as if it were my own company.

At the same time that I was creating ways to increase the business for this location, I was also dealing with my own personal businesses. After my third house acquisition, I moved into the last purchase and settled there as my primary home, while the other two became rental properties. In terms of my maintenance company, I had several contracts with logistics companies, Hometown Buffet, and an apartment complex close to Beverly Hills. Although my own business seemed to be going well, the reality was the opposite. My business partner was stealing from me. He was collecting payments, and before I knew it, disappeared with it all. I was stuck with no money to pay my employees, so I had no option but to use my own money to pay them (remember, never burn your bridges). I was forced to cancel all the contracts and close the company down. While not easy, it was the right decision. I needed to focus on my rental properties and on taking care of my career, as it had skyrocketed over the previous couple of years.

In my late twenties, I had two more experiences that I want to share with you. First, I made several business trips to Mexico as well as a personal business trip to South America (Colombia), which was a one-of-a-kind opportunity. First of all, I was able to take this trip because I was building relationships with customers as well as my vendors while working both my full-time job as well as my side business. Not only did I create good synergy with one specific vendor, I became good friends with him, and he invited me to his home town to spend time with his family. I was blessed to have gotten this great opportunity from a great friend who continues to be a great friend to this day. Sometimes, people do not understand how critical it is to create strong connections and build rapport. You just never know where you can end up or what kind of long-term friendship you might have with a person who crosses your path.

"I think if I've learned anything about friendship, it's to hang in, stay connected, fight for them, and let them fight for you. Don't walk away, don't be distracted, don't be too busy or tired, don't take them for granted. Friends are part of the glue that holds life and faith together. Powerful stuff."

—*Jon Katz*

My second experience came from different type of relationship, one where we started as co-workers, became friends, and ultimately ended up in a romantic relationship. After approximately four years living the single life, I found the person who fulfilled my life. Her name is Tal, and our romantic relationship began with the purpose of uniting our lives. I was truly blessed, my life seemed to have taken a good turn. I had a good job, was involved in the real estate investing, had a loving girlfriend, knew my daughter was doing great, knew my family was good, and had a good number of friends. A few months into my relationship with Tal, she moved in and our relationship became more official and committed. The best thing that happened to us was that we were there to support each other, and from that point, we were partners through all of our life events and moves.

There are several lessons I hope you'll take from all of these experiences. They all revolve around never giving up, no matter when the world screams out to you that isn't possible and no matter what wrong path it tries to take you down. Although I am sharing with you my life experiences from my youth to my late twenties, there are many examples and triggers that any of you can relate to no matter your current situation or age. As you can see, life has given me many turns, but I had a great passion. Even though I had to cross over boundaries (and I did, multiple times), learn a new language, go through several jobs, face humiliation, or lose my identity, I never gave up. I continued to educate myself and do whatever it took to stand out. I took many risks and fell many times, and I got up and did it again. As my mentor, Marshall Sylver, says, "Rehearse, review, revise" until you get it right, and be certain of the outcome. As you look at your life and notice that you are still alive, recognize that your time here is not over yet, so make the best out of it.

> "Fail early, fail often, but always fail forward."
> —*John C. Maxwell*

Keep going, and do not stop. Do not let anything or anyone get in the way of your success or create any obstacles between you and being satisfied and wealthy in your own particular way.

PART IV

MIDDLE ADULTHOOD

16

FAIL, BUT DON'T GIVE UP

H ave you ever heard of an investment going bad? As I think about it, there are no bad investments, as every investment is already risky. We don't make bad investments, we just sometimes make investments without all the necessary knowledge and tools to ensure that they're educated investments.

As I entered my thirties, I came to the realization that I was not fully educated when it came to real estate investing. I thought I had made good moves, yet as the US housing bubble started to decline in 2006 and 2007, without adequate knowledge or help from other experts, I neglected to see any real signs that something bad was about to happen to the real estate market. The bursting of the housing bubble was a major contribution to the 2007-2009 recession that took place in the US, forcing many homeowners and investors (especially new investors) to lose out on their real estate investments.

I only mention this to put my next major experience into perspective. Although I was still making real estate purchases all the way through 2007 and still buying during the market peak, I also had to face difficult times with my properties. By 2010, I was facing a short sale and had started a foreclosure on a second property. My largest challenge at that time was a lack of steady income from renters. The housing bubble also impacted thousands of jobs and made it difficult for people to sustain not only their primary homes but also stay on top of their rent. Getting into desperation mode and doing whatever I could, I took on any tenant just to get that one month's rent to pay the mortgage. This too was an uneducated mistake because I found myself bringing unqualified people into my properties—people who did not pay rent on time and brought more tenant challenges to me. Because I live in a tenant friendly state, not a landlord friendly state, it would take forever to evict these people.

As time went by, and after multiple tenants in each of my first two properties as well as many break-ins from homeless people who would steal from and vandalize my properties, I came to a point where I could no longer sustain these properties. I finally decided to get some professional help and pay a company to help me with loan modification. Unfortunately, I hired the wrong company, and they took advantage of people (as did many companies during the housing bubble), taking their money even before helping or creating a positive outcome.

Not having too many other options, I successfully came to an agreement with one of my mortgage companies (after almost a year and a half) and agreed on a short sale price. In 2011, I lost one of my properties. The bank did not want to work with me on the second property, and later in the year, I foreclosed on that investment. This was devastating because for the next ten years I knew I lost the ability to leverage any type of credit for a large purchase. The one thing I did correctly was protect my personal home. I was not about to lose that property and put my family out on the streets. I made sure I kept up with the mortgage payments, even though my home's value dropped from its original purchase price by approximately $125,000.

Two other major events took place in my family during this time as well. Neither one of them was a bad experience; one was expected and the other was a life-changing event. First, my daughter turned fifteen years old, and as it is for many Hispanic families, it was my pleasure to give my daughter a celebration that I hope she will forever remember. This event was planned for several weeks, and going from a childhood having nothing to being able to provide this celebration for my daughter was a complete blessing. I never had the ability to celebrate any of my childhood birthdays the way we celebrate my daughter's birthdays. For a Hispanic family—mostly for the parents—the fifteenth birthday is a day to remember and it meant a lot, especially since she is my only daughter.

The second major event took place several months later, and before I share it with you, I want to tell you a bit about my daughter. She is very similar to me, and at the time she was a dedicated student going to Hollywood High, not involved with any negative influences, with a promising future. She is a hard worker, always helping me without worrying about breaking a nail. I truly felt and feel blessed to call her my daughter.

Fast-forward several months after her fifteenth birthday when I was asked to come to a meeting at Mona's house. As I entered the house, the unexpected happened. There were several people in the room, and I could already tell that something was happening. Sure enough, the bomb was dropped on me that my daughter was expecting a baby. I did not know what to say or how to react, and interestingly, Mona didn't know how I was going to react, given that I have only one daughter. I've always been tough on my daughter. Therefore, Mona was prepared to get or call anyone necessary depending upon my reaction. At that moment, there was much confusion, and was hard to accept the fact that my daughter was going to be a teen parent.

I did not react in a negative way. Instead, I embraced and accepted the reality that the only option I had was to support, give, and provide for my daughter. I remembered when I was in her shoes, when I was facing the same reality, and my parents did not abandon me. They opened their arms to help me. I realized that I couldn't turn my back on her. I had to support her and continue to teach her based on my own experiences, and help her overcome any obstacles. Life has so much negativity, and people often put you down and judge you because they have nothing better to do. I was not going to leave my daughter alone on this journey. Although I was upset, I was ready to be part of her journey. Since I had always been strict, I strongly requested that my daughter move into my house as her primary home (Mona and I were still alternating weekends and days), and to this date, she is still living with me.

In July 2012, my daughter gave birth to my very lovable grandson. It was critical that my daughter kept up with her studies and finished school on time, which she did and finished as an honor student. It was also important that my grandson was raised with values and principles, which he was, and he has a bright future ahead of him. Finally, this event officially made me the youngest grandfather I've ever known, and I'm very grateful and happy in that role.

As my family grew, there were so many other priorities and focuses to take care of that part of me was relieved that I was finished dealing with evictions, bad tenants, banks, and people who had no interest in helping others and were only looking to take advantage of people.

This gave me the opportunity to assess my real estate investments, and I came to the realization that I was moving too fast while in my twenties. The issue wasn't only that I was moving too fast—in fact, I encourage you to take risks and make investments without being afraid. However, be sure that, before taking them and making them, you educate yourself so that you clearly understand what you are getting into. Although I had really good intentions, I made the mistake of not leveraging the knowledge of others who had been in the business longer than I had. Part of the issue was that I did not know any, or at least I could not find them in my circle or nearby circle of friends. Here are some lessons learned in terms of what I should have done differently:

1. Prior to making any real estate investment, educate yourself on rental properties
2. Educate yourself on the landlord and tenant laws in your state and county.
3. Hire a realtor who has an interest in you, and buy low as an investment, not at retail price
4. Understand the CAP Rate on the property
5. Stop doing things yourself, hire a property management company to handle your property (or properties). There are many advantages to doing this, including the fact that they run background checks and maintain your property, collect rent, handle evictions, manage your budget, ensure your property is rented as much as possible, review financials, and understand if

you have the financials to make your next rental investment.

6. Review location, location, location

I believe that if I would have done all of this, I would still have my properties and probably many more. I am also thankful that I was able to experience this firsthand, as it gave me the opportunity to share my experience with others and give you a starting point if you are looking to invest in real estate "buy and hold."

Because of this experience, I decided to focus solely on my career. I had the pleasure of learning a lot more about running a business, looking at the financials, and finding profit opportunities. At the same time, I was enhancing my leadership skills by mentoring and managing a group of people, and I was building many relationships with vendors and customers. I was also given the opportunity to travel both nationally and internationally with the company.

On top of that, I continued traveling for my own pleasure, and always traveled with Tal and my daughter (always thinking of giving my daughter the life I never had). In order to further expand my business knowledge, I made the decision to shift educational knowledge and decided to pursue my masters degree in business. I figured that although my previous education was in IT, the best option for me was to go back and focus on business. Ultimately, I was managing a company, and I'd also had experience running my own businesses. I knew I needed a better understanding of the fundamental principles of running and managing a business, which led me to enroll in the masters degree program.

Going back to school was demanding, especially when my job also demanded ten- to twelve-hour work days, including some weekends. Not only did my job demand quite a bit of me, school did as well. There was a lot of material to read, many essays to write, and many projects to complete. While attending school, I got close to some of my classmates who, like myself, were looking to grow toward a better future. They were like-minded individuals full of aspirations and goals for the future. Those are the kind of people you want to be around—people who can help you by pushing you to become a better version of yourself.

After much hard work, dedication, long nights, and the strong desire to further my education, I had the pleasure of graduating at the end of 2012 with my MBA (Master of Business Administration). This was a huge accomplishment for me. With a successful career, an awesome family, and a great partner next to my side, I had no complaints whatsoever.

> "Achievement seems to be connected with action.
> Successful men and women keep moving. They make
> mistakes, but they don't quit."
> —*Conrad Hilton*

Not only did I receive a higher education, I also put into practice what I learned, which gave me a better foundation to manage the standalone building I was responsible for. On top of that, my entrepreneurial mindset compelled me to give another of my own companies a shot, and I opened my second maintenance company. I finally felt equipped to run a solid business. I knew that to stay competitive and gain more business I needed to focus a lot of my time in sales and building business relationships. With the help of my business partner, who also happened to be my girlfriend (Tal), we were able to secure a few contracts that kept us in business for a little while.

That said, we did not have the type of growth we were hoping for, and our lack of knowledge of the maintenance industry, the different permits we needed to have, and the small profit margins made our decision to close down the business and move on to the next best thing quite easy.

As you recognize the different businesses I've been involved with and had to close as well as the job accomplishments I have made, it is important to take into consideration that in order to succeed in this life, you must continue to do the things that others are not willing to do. It often requires not giving up the first, second, or third time when none of the businesses result in the outcome you were hoping for. As my mentor, Marshall Sylver, repeats time after time, "Keep throwing noodles to the wall until one of them sticks..." Simply never give up, because one failed business does not mean that all businesses will fail.

"If you've failed, that means you're doing something. If you're doing something, you have a chance."
—*Robert Kiyosaki*

It is not only the new or small companies that have to make difficult decisions to reinvent or create better opportunities for financial growth. The company I was working for decided to close down my location and consolidate operations from Gardena, California to Carson, California. After five years with this company, I had grown enough professionally that I was ready to take on any challenge and opportunity put in front of me. Due to my long-lasting relationship with my employees, vendors, customers, and superiors, I was given the opportunity to manage a larger location with a more complex mix of clients and different product offerings worldwide.

This was not only a change to a bigger location, it also meant more pay with more responsibilities and a lot more exposure. And I was all ready to tackle this new chapter of my life head-on.

17

LOSING A GREAT WOMAN

Entering 2014, at just thirty-four years old, I had overcome many things, despite life putting many obstacles in front of me and telling this immigrant kid that his dreams weren't possible. I was in a good place. I was happy to have been given the opportunity to have taken a five-generation family picture, something I deeply cherish, and I hoped there were many more years to come.

Yet again, life's obstacles got in the way. This time, it was not related to work or to me directly, but it touched me deep down in my heart. My grandma, who I grew up with, who raised me, who worked side-by-side with me to give me the life I have, got pretty sick and had several small heart attacks. These were some very scary moments, and for a second, I thought I had lost her.

The entire family made a point to go see her at the hospital to provide moral and family support. Indeed, it was a scare, but it was not her time. She was a strong woman and was able to recover from these small heart attacks. She was released from the hospital.

Given my grandma's condition and the fact that her

hospital was close to my house, my parents and grandma moved into my home temporarily while my grandma recovered. During their stay, my grandma was facing ups and downs, filled with energy some days and other days drained. It was great to have my parents and grandma stay with me along with my grandkid, daughter, and Tal. Unfortunately, I was not thrilled by the reasons that brought us all under one roof.

Things seemed to be somewhat normal, my grandma was going through a recovery period, and part of the family discussions included the idea that perhaps she would not be with us for too much longer. I felt disbelief and deep down, I could not accept that this could happen to me, to my family. I did not want to accept that her death was a possibility. Because of the multiple heart attacks, it was hard for my grandma to move and stand up, so my parents brought in a special bed and made my living room their home.

One day, early in the morning (at approximately 5:30am), all I could hear from my room was a loud scream. At that moment, my heart stopped. I got out of bed and ran into the living room to find my mom over my grandma's chest, crying. My grandma (the woman I called "Ama") had passed away. My mom witnessed the very minute my grandma's soul separated from her body, which was exactly the moment my mom screamed so loudly and continued to cry out. At that moment, everyone in the house—my parents, daughter, grandkid, Tal, and I—stood in the living room in tears. We had just lost a great woman.

Abraham Lincoln said, "All that I am or hope to be, I owe to my angel mother." I am blessed to have had two of them, and one of my angels had just left this world. September 28, 2014 was a very difficult day for my family, and during her funeral we had so many people come and share their condolences with us. My older brother and his wife flew in from Oklahoma to be there, and one of my grandma's nieces was there too. Several of my friends shared this moment with my family, providing moral support.

For the first time in my life, I'd lost a very special and close person to me. I know for a fact that I have come this far because of her teachings, her dedication, and her refusal to ever give up. Regardless of the small jobs we had or whether we had money or food, she never gave up. Those experiences gave me my drive, my determination, my ambition, my mojo to fight for a better life, even when life got in the way.

I knew that if I would have given up after her passing, I would not just fail myself but I would fail her too. We'd come too far to stop. I had to get back up again, put myself back together, and focus on what I still had to make the best of it for my family and for her.

Working with a worldwide company and looking at the national and global opportunities, I had no hesitation about proving to my superiors that I was able and willing to take on more challenges, because that is what I was taught by my grandma. Always with that hungry mind, I went to work seeking the next great opportunity. I was searching for a way to grow within the industry of logistics at my current company. I was able to connect to top people in the company, from the regional manager to the VPs and CEO. One of my objectives was to show that I was disciplined, dedicated, and educated.

With numerous years of schooling under my belt, I was a firm believer in traditional school and will always encourage anyone to follow the traditional approach of going to school, getting a great education, and landing a great job at a top corporation. I encourage this, as my success is a product of this concept. However, I wanted more than just the traditional approach. I applied for several positions within the company, with some of the positions in different cities, and even after showing up and proving myself, I was, for the first time, denied potential growth.

Although I received really good feedback from my superiors, I did not get the promotions I went after. Part of me thought that perhaps it simply was not yet my time to make my next career move. Or, was that just a limiting belief I told myself? The answer depends on what came afterward.

"Your level of belief in yourself will inevitably manifest itself in whatever you do."
—*Les Brown*

As you assess your current situation, take into account whether you are creating limiting beliefs or are truly working toward your next breakthrough. The reality is, if you are giving yourself limiting beliefs, you need to stop that. Stay focused and motivated, and have a can-do attitude. If it is not your time, ensure that you continue to work on yourself until you get what you want. Don't stop or give up.

Understanding this concept and putting it into practice, I continued to work on my development, continued to show up to work, and continued to provide value to my employer. I knew that as long as I continued to be persistent, my next career move was just around the corner. An important part of my role was the ability to be a leader, to develop my team and provide direction for them to grow within each of their own careers. I am pleased to say that there were several people (my little brother being one of them, as he worked for me for several years) who followed instructions and allowed me to lead them. It resulted not only in their growth but it also gave me the ability to expand my leadership skills to prepare for the future.

Sure enough, I was given an upward mobility career opportunity to be in charge of a particular product for the company by leading a district. This was not necessarily the corporate job I was seeking, yet it was still a step up. Small steps lead to big steps, and this promotion was just one of those small steps toward the bigger one. With this promotion, I was responsible for putting together financial reports to open up new locations. By the time these places were up and running, I was in charge of leading four facilities (Gardena, Carson, Rancho Dominguez, and San Diego). Further, my team was expanded by the addition of more leaders, and we hired new employees from blue collar to white collar to supervisors and management. This also gave me the ability to promote people who embraced my leadership and mentoring. Not only did this open opportunities for me but it also opened opportunities for others.

I was balancing my work life with my personal life, still recovering from my grandma's loss, content to have a grandkid, a loving daughter, a caring girlfriend, an awesome family (parents and brothers), and great childhood memories with my grandma. I made several trips outside the states to enjoy time away from work and this thing we call life. It is important to find that balance, and just as you work hard, always ensure that you make time to play even harder.

18

TRANSFORMATION

B y now you have surely come to realize that seeking for more and searching for your true journey is not an easy path to take. Yet, when you badly want it, you have to fight for it. No matter who gets in your way or who tells you that you can't or what life throws at you, if it is your desire to seek greatness, it is your responsibility to never give up.

2016 was a year of realization, a year of change. I had faced so many challenges, yet believe it or not, I still felt that something was missing. It was the year that I made a commitment to myself that I had to make a change, a change like none I'd made before.

My job was demanding much more from me, and I could see many changes taking place. People who had been with the company for a long time and who held key top positions were getting laid off. I witnessed long-time co-workers being removed from payroll, and the interesting thing was that this was not happening just in this company. It was happening in almost all the companies I had worked for. The only reason why this was clear to me was because this was the company I had been with for over nine years. My very first encounter was when I got laid off due to an acquisition taking place. From there, I took part in several companies, yet my focus was my career and my studies, so I did not pay attention to the signs that people were losing their jobs. This even happened in my own family, when my older brother—who is well overqualified for his job—lost his corporate position along with another 1,000-plus employees due to financial cuts. Seeing long hours at work without a bright future, I found myself questioning my career and life again, wondering to myself, "Is this how life will be, moving from job to job, never truly having a secure job that I can call home?"

I was so glad for Tal, who encouraged us to go to a real estate seminar, a seminar where the material would cover investing. I was a bit cynical since the first time around my real estate investing was not successful. Nevertheless, we both attended the seminar in the Los Angeles area, and after getting the basics of real estate investing, we both agreed that this was the answer we were seeking. I particularly felt that this was it, given that it seemed my career was not going anywhere. This gave me a different perspective and lured me back into the investing world. Tal and I took another risk and made a financial investment to get educated on how to become successful real estate investors.

Several weeks later, we attended our first three-day class. This was for sure a different type of education, nothing like any of my degrees or traditional school, yet there was a lot of valuable information provided and we continued to invest in our real estate education. Shortly thereafter, we opened up a company together called C2 Real Estate Investments, LLC (for company information, you can visit www.c2realestateinvestments.com). Still working my full-time job, I shifted my priorities and attention little by little to make our real estate company successful.

Because I had decided to shift gears, my focus at my full-time job was diminishing, and my interest in it was dying down. Not long after, I left the company that I'd worked for almost ten years and joined another logistics company. This was a great jump into a promising career. That opportunity I was looking for finally came around. I was in charge of all customer contracts, engineering, project management, innovative solutions, and division marketing. Best of all, it was a corporate job, and I was responsible for all US locations. This was the dream job I was hoping to get at my previous company (that came to me a bit too late), however by the time I got it, my focus had shifted toward making my real estate business work. The irony of this is that the dream job I was seeking for two years prior finally came, except it was no longer the dream job.

I worked at this new company for a period of two years, and a few months past the two-year mark I took the leap of faith and left my well-paid and very rewarding job to go one hundred percent into real estate investing and become a full-time entrepreneur.

"If you want to be successful you have to jump, there's no way around it. If you're safe, you'll never soar."
—*Steve Harvey*

"The most successful people in this world recognize that taking chances to get what they want is much more productive than sitting around being too scared to take a shot. "
—*Steve Harvey*

During 2016, Tal and I focused on continuous non-traditional education for real estate, and at the same time we were working on setting up the foundation for our business. With the mission of making this business grow, it was critical to set it up properly, to treat it as a successful and high-revenue business even if, at that time, it was not yet producing. I worked on making sure there was a business account, a virtual office, marketing tools in place, a business structure (both operationally and for marketing), and a business that was ready to produce.

19

MINDSET SHIFT

After going to many classes and seminars and setting up the business structure, I had one of my first clarity moments regarding knowledge and education. For my entire life, I was programmed to think that the best reward one can have is to go to college, get an education, and secure a good job. I'm still a firm believer in education; I knew I had to get a degree to get that dream job. However, this time around I had a mindset shift.

I've learned more about life, finances, business, and growth through the seminars I was attending than I did through my MBA program. I still believe in and support education, and I know it's important for anyone to be educated, except my mindset shift was with regard to getting educated the *non-traditional* way. You can often get more from classroom seminars like the ones I've attended than you can from traditional school. Robert Kiyosaki talks a lot about financial education and literacy and understanding money—something that is not taught in traditional schools—and the reason that the majority of the population comes out with a degree, seeking a job with a huge debt for an education that does not promise a career. This mindset shift became more evident as I took a different path in my life.

> "Because students leave school without financial skills, millions of educated people pursue their profession successfully, but later find themselves struggling financially."
> ——*Robert Kiyosaki*

By end of 2016, I had traveled all over the world (including Spain, France, Rome, Honduras, Colombia, Belize, and Croatia, just to name a few), had a master's degree, had a family, had enough money to stay above water, had worked for an established company, and now had a new promising business for which I had much hope.

As I entered 2017, I had one mission in mind and that was to grow my real estate business. Part of my challenge was that, because I was initially still working a full-time job while growing my real estate business, I wasn't getting the type of rapid success and growth I was looking for. Another challenge I faced was that, with my new corporate job, my responsibilities had tripled. I was not only putting together a new department, I was also traveling a lot, and when I was home, the only time I had time to work on my own business was from 6:00pm until I fell asleep. This was also the case for Tal (who was not just my girlfriend but also my business partner). She had also gotten a promotion and was working even longer hours than I was. Our jobs made it difficult to focus on strategic plans to grow the real estate business. But we refused to give up.

Understanding that we needed to get more exposure by getting more leads, and that the key to doing that was getting our name out to the market, we went to Open Houses, monthly REI Club meetings, and otherwise networked as much as we could during every moment we were in public. It still wasn't enough, and by that point we had invested so much money into the business that frustration began to set in, and the thought of not taking this business anywhere was haunting me more and more. I began to have limiting beliefs that we would actually come out winning. Even after countless hours of hard work, putting into practice some very common practices in real estate investing such as sending mailers to owners of vacant houses, sending mailers to absentee owners, cold calling from different sources such as Craigslist, using Bandit signs, networking on REIC, networking at open houses, placing ads on social media, reviewing properties out of the MLS, and creating forms on REI software and platforms, we weren't growing fast enough.

Although we had done some wholesales and flips, it was not enough, and our financial cushion was running low. This was very frustrating and only led to arguments, disagreements, and disconnection between Tal and me. As we continued to find ways to improve our business model, we were able to secure tickets to another three-day seminar taking place at the Los Angeles Convention Center. I knew that it was time to go back and learn more business principles, network as much as possible (given this was an event for over 5,000 people), and listen to some of the most successful people in the industry as well as people who went from nothing to a fortune. Those in attendance included Pit Bull, Magic Johnson, Suze Orman, Tony Robbins, Marshall Sylver, and Sylvester Stallone.

This Real Estate Wealth Expo had many keynote speakers and thousands of real estate professionals for us to network with. It was exactly what we needed, or at least it was exactly what I needed. My relationship with Tal was deteriorating.

After seeing so many great speakers, there was one in particular who we had seen perform the day before. He did an entertaining hypnosis show, and his name was Marshall Sylver. Not knowing much about this entertainer, his show was so good that we were excited to see him the next day. And let me tell you, this guy was able to close very easily hundreds of people at a three-day, self-development seminar called The Turning Point. I was one of them. I loved what he was teaching, and I knew I wanted more. For those who know me, I am not easily amused and do not buy into a product or service I do not believe in, but something told me I needed this for the expansion of my business.

Two weeks later, I attend The Turning Point. Tal was sick and was not able to make it for the first two days. Let me tell you, the teachings, the networking, and the materials were unbelievable. On Day Three (Tal joined for the last day) I knew I needed more; I needed to connect with Marshall. As a matter of fact, there were a few things he said that made me think and influenced my next decision.

He said, "The fastest way to change something is to get a mentor; it is the fastest way to massive results." Given my experience with him at the Real Estate Wealth Expo and my experience at his Turning Point event, I had a desire to get him to be my mentor. I brought this up to Tal, and given that we were already struggling financially, she pretty much left it up to me. On the third day of The Turning Point, and for the first time in my life, I made a decision to get him as my mentor and paid $50,000 to have him on my team. The only downside was that the next mentoring program, which would be held at his Las Vegas residence, was not going to happen for another three months. Although I had no choice but to wait, I really needed that mentoring program *at that moment* to make major change in my real estate business.

As we continued to struggle, not only were we not communicating as a couple or business partners but the financial burden pulled us further apart. All the pressure, the setbacks, the business not producing as expected, and not having the necessary financial support made me break down, and for the first time in my relationship with Tal, I went to a dark place. From that point, my relationship with Tal went down the drain, and on New Year's Day, 2018, my nine-year relationship with her ended.

Just when I thought things could not get any worse, they did. The one person who, at one point, I thought I would spend the rest of my life with was no longer with me, and the only thing we had together was our business. With this major shift in my life, I knew I had to re-evaluate and make a change. The first change was to attend my mentoring program and learn as much as possible from it. I could not wait to be part of it.

20

THE TURNING POINT

A t the end of February 2018, I finally had the opportunity to see Marshall again at his mansion, and let me tell you, I thought I had seen everything. This, however, was beyond my expectations, not only because of his mansion and the opportunity to see him as a human being, a normal person with a loving family, but also to see his passion to help each and every one of the mentoring students.

"You are one certain idea away from a billion dollars."
—Marshall Sylver

The three days were very well spent, and having that opportunity to get a one-on-one evaluation of my business and life gave me a sense of accomplishment and further ideas to develop my business. What was great was that, from this mentoring program, I truly came out having my own mentor who would work with me moving forward, and that was exactly what I needed, especially given the emotional roller coaster I'd been on.

After attending my mentoring session, I knew I had to re-invent myself. I knew I had to do something that I had never done in order to succeed. As I think about it now, this was the beginning of my own turning point in life, the beginning of what I now know to be my ultimate phase in life.

I knew I had come a long way. I had made my own success. I had traveled all over the world. I had accomplished so much professionally and educationally. I had a beautiful daughter and grandkid and loving parents. However, something deep down in my heart told me this was not all there was—there was much more, a bigger purpose, and with that thought, I started changing my thinking and my focus and began to slowly make changes in my day-to-day life.

One of those changes came when I was first introduced to the book *The Miracle Morning* by Hal Elrod (which I highly recommend). In this book, I found material and information that I put into practice. Material such as a full assessment of my life (appropriately called the Wheel of Life assessment) whereby you grade yourself in ten areas of your life, from spiritual to finances to self-development. By doing this exercise, I discovered that I needed to improve many areas in my life, areas where I didn't think I needed any further improvement. Continuing to learn through this book, I had so many clarity moments, and one that resonated with me was when Elrod said, "Remember, the moment you accept total responsibility for everything in your life is the moment you claim the power to change anything in your life."

I knew I had to take ownership of my life, and more importantly I had to take responsibility *for* my life, regardless of my past experiences, regardless of what I did or who did what to me. I also came to the realization that I had to work on myself and not just my business. I had to fix myself first, everything else will follow.

I had to work on myself by educating my mind, by creating habits and rituals and working on my wheel of life. Instead of wasting time doing non-productive, non-income-generating activities on my daily life, I was on a mission to do things that would bring daily *value* to my life.

I have attended numerous seminars and events held by Marshall Sylver, and I have learned so much that has helped me during my transformation phase. One major change was the ability to surrender and change the programs in my mind.

When I look at Marshall's advice and read *The Miracle Morning*, when I listen to people like Jim Rohn, Les Brown, and Tony Robbins, I find many commonalities such as consistency in reading, in habits, in programming, and in being part of a like-minded community.

I've tried to read in the past, except I rarely finished a book and never felt the passion to really read. The last time I read and actually finished a book was in high school, and the only reason I did was because it was a requirement. However, after committing to making a change, I decided to include reading in my daily life. I even found myself doing things I would never before do when it came to reading. I remember a time when I was traveling for business, and while I was at the airport waiting for my flight, I noticed that I would soon finish with the current book I was reading. So, without hesitation, I actually stepped into the airport bookstore and picked up Tony Robbins' *Unshakeable*.

Speaking of reading material, within *The Miracle Morning* Hal Elrod refers to another great book, which I ended up picking up and reading. I also highly recommend it. The book is *Think & Grow Rich* by Napoleon Hill. This book contains many exercises that also help in refocusing your life, many of which I practice on a daily basis. Other books I recommend are *The compound Effect* by Darren Hardy, *The 4-Hour Work Week* by Timothy Ferriss, *Rich Dad's Cashflow Quadrant* by Robert Kiyosaki, and Millionaire Success Habits: The Gateway to Wealth and Prosperity by Dean Graziosi.

As I continued to make breakthroughs in my life and continued to focus on transforming my life, I made several other changes. I want to address two major mistakes made by so many people that force them to accept life for what it is or never get out from under their old ways—things I've decided to change, as I was also guilty of making these mistakes.

One of the reasons why people cannot move forward and instead continue returning to the same place is that many people get caught up in the past. The past is merely that: the past. Yet many people have what Hal Elrod refers to "rear mirror syndrome" whereby they tend to allow the past to overpower their present and future capabilities.

When people are faced with challenges, the first place to seek validation is past experiences. To move forward in life, we simply need to leave the past in the past and not limit ourselves to what could have potentially been. Just because something happened or did not work in the past does not mean it will have the same result in the future. I also believe that the past is a lesson. What took place is gone, and it cannot be redone and or recreated. However, one can learn, grow, and make the necessary changes to ensure that they don't make the same mistakes. Your past does not determine your future or path; don't allow this syndrome to overpower you.

"We mistakenly believe that who we *were* is who we *are*,

> thus limiting our true potential in the present, based on the
> limitations of our past."
> —*Hal Elrod*

The other thing that holds people back is accepting life events and present circumstances as a result of one's destiny. While it might be, many people tend to misinterpret situations. The idea that "things happen for a reason" is not entirely true. The fact that you are no longer together with someone or you did not get that raise or were laid off may have been (or still be) controllable. Yes, you can be influenced by others talking to you, by others feeding certain programs to you, by observing people around you, through your own spiritual faith, or by any other means that help you direct and or shift your thoughts. But at the end of the day, you have the ability and power to embrace any of those influences and ultimately make a decision as to the outcome. It is wrong to utilize the phrase "things happen for a reason" as an excuse not to change or take full responsibility and control of your outcomes. Even if things *did* happen for a reason, it is critical not to let a situation put you into a comfort zone or into a "can't do" attitude where you do nothing to improve your situation.

> "It is often said that everything happens for a reason, but
> you must embrace the perspective that it's never a reason
> that is predetermined or out of your control."
> —*Hal Elrod*

Because of the teachings I was getting from reading and attending seminars, I had some difficult decisions to make in order to be able to be fully engaged and focused while going through my transformation period. Below are some things I had to change, things and principles that anyone looking to make a change in life must also make:

1. I decided to get rid of any negative programming from cable television (I discontinued my service).
2. I decided to stop wasting time and making the best use of my time by not watching TV shows, movies, or any other content on TV that did not improve my current situation. (Instead, I watched documentaries or motivational videos like *The Secret* or programs related to real estate investing.)
3. I decided to let go of listening to radio stations while driving. Instead, I listen to motivational videos, eBooks (enhancing my thoughts and providing ideas to improve my life and business), or a positive programming CD (for example, Marshall Sylver's Irresistible Influence).
4. I put into practice each and every day the lifesaving principles found in *The Miracle Morning.*
5. Silence, Meditate, Pray
6. Affirmations
7. Visualization
8. Exercise
9. Read
10. Journaling
11. I read out loud affirmations twice a day, every day (influenced by *The Secret* and *Think and Grow Rich*).
12. I created two visions boars (influenced by *The Secret* and *The Miracle Morning*).

13. I read daily to improve my programming and thinking.
14. I found and got involved with a local church group to get more spiritually focused.
15. I attend self-development and business development seminars as often as possible such as The Turning Point by Marshall Sylver (good for personal development, networking with business owners, and like-minded people).

Going through this transformation was not easy, making these changes in my life was different than ever before and required great effort, especially when life, my comfort zone, doubts, the world's questions and no's came between doing and not doing these habits each day. Overcoming the laziness and procrastination of not doing these things made the difference between transforming and not transforming.

"Don't wish it was easier, wish you were better. Don't wish for less problems, wish for more skills. Don't wish for less challenges, wish for more wisdom."
—*Jim Rohn*

21

CONTINUING FORWARD

A s I continue to work on myself, network with other people, and join ventures with other business owners, I learn to become a better business man and entrepreneur. As I continue to go to seminars and have the good fortune to spend time networking and connecting with business people as well as the pleasure of connecting with millionaires (Dean Graziosi, Marshall Sylver, and Cody Sperber, to name a few), I continue to learn an important point about business and wealth. Many of these people talk about having multiple streams of income. The Millionaire Mentor says that "the average millionaire has seven sources of income."

As a result, I continue to enhance my real estate investing business and make additional investments into programs from Clever Investor, create marketing ads, build business credit, and participate in joint ventures with other investors. On top of that, I got involved in other businesses to create additional streams of income (some of those to include residual income). By the time I was finished investing, in addition to my primary company (C2 Real

Estate Investments), I've opened up a money company business of ATMs, a business with a video marketing platform, a business in vacation giveaways, a weight management company, and a consulting business for the logistics industry. One of the benefits of all these businesses is that they all work together, and with many of them, I was able to get a customer from a customer. Also, getting involved in and opening these companies positioned me on the right side of the quadrant, the B and I (to learn more about the left and right side of the quadrant, read *Rich Dad's Cashflow Quadrant* by Robert Kiyosaki).

With the mindset shift, proper programming, necessary actions, and spending time with people who are smarter than I am, I am certain that I am setting up my life for success. You have the same choice. Hopefully, this book has inspired you to do the same.

"Action is the foundational key to all success."
—*Pablo Picasso*

AFTERWORD

NEVER LET YOUR GUARD DOWN

Whether or not you let it get to you when life hits you in the face or the world is giving up on you is entirely dependent upon your determination to take action.

I decided to write this book not only to share my personal experiences from family, education, and career but also (and more importantly) to share my commitment to never giving up. Throughout my many life challenges, I've realized some very important things that everyone has to do to ensure that they keep moving forward toward a rewarding life.

Whether you are looking to improve your professional or personal life (or both), there are several things you need to take into consideration, and more importantly, act upon. It all starts with you. Neither the world nor your spouse nor your parents nor the economy nor politics can hold you back. Only you can.

One area to improve is your programming and mind triggers. Just like a healthy diet, it's your choice whether or not you are feeding your stomach healthy food to keep up your energy, maintain your weight, and get all the necessary minerals and vitamins. Similar to the diet you feed your body, you need to feed your mind with the right type of food, including positive thoughts, (positive affirmations), the right type of programming (motivational videos and audios), and the right type of triggers (instead of seeing something as a problem or an issue, set is as a challenge). You also must continue to educate your mind (not with traditional schooling) in terms of personal growth, business growth, finances, dealing with people, and no longer focusing on limitations.

Develop daily affirmations. Some of my own are:

- I am unstoppable
- I am entrepreneurial
- I am successful
- I am healthy
- I am spiritually sound and focus
- I am surrounded by love
- I am rich
- I am wanted
- I am loved
- I am happy
- I am blessed
- I am at peace with everything and everyone
- I attract new clients every day
- I am attractive
- I wake up happy and excited every single day
- I have a lot of money
- I am helpful
- I am a great partner
- I am wealthy
- I am abundant

- I am beautiful
- I am committed
- I am generous and helpful
- I am kind and loving
- I am confident
- I am strong
- I am certain
- I am grateful
- I am deserving of all my dreams
- I love my life
- I am fearless
- I am a millionaire

I highly recommend that you create the discipline to write down your own affirmations and read them each day with passion, out loud in front of a mirror. Read them twice a day, once when you wake up and once before you go to sleep.

Another area to improve is your physiology. When you combine your mind triggers with your physiology and act as if what you desire is real, what you see in your mind and the way you act in real life will eventually become one. Your physiology plays an important role in your daily life. For example, any business revolves around sales and people. If you are approachable, your business will flourish. If you are not approachable, your business will suffer. A person is approachable because of his character, physiology, and way of thinking.

As you focus on your personal development, focus on the right type of education. I am a firm believer in getting a good education, however given my own experience, I do not encourage traditional school only. The only time I do suggest it is for mere self-accomplishment. Many millionaires did not finish school, and those who did still went back to get further non-traditional education to excel in both their personal and professional lives. Non-traditional education includes:

- Educational Seminars (in sales, real estate, MLMs, finances, etc.)
- Get a mentor (**so important**, someone to teach you and hold you accountable)
- Join entrepreneurial communities
- Join accountability groups
- Join positive and certain groups (e.g. The Miracle Morning community)
- Workshops (hands-on)

"I never let schooling interface with my education."
—*Mark Twain*

As you get ready to make changes in your life and take control of your future and destiny as I did, create new habits—activities that are not just a one-day activity or something you do every so often. Instead, create habits that become a ritual—they'll get done without you even thinking about them. The vast majority of people do not wake up or go to sleep asking, "Do I feel like brushing my teeth?" This action is an automatic habit and ritual. In the same way this was taught to us, we need to develop habits to improve our situation. We need habits such as:

- Exercise daily
- Set daily targets (goals)
- Be specific and precise (date and timeframe)
- Break down and understand all the steps
- Create a checklist
- Delegate as much as possible (know what is the

best use of your time), only focus on those
things that are moving you forward
- Attend as many networking events as you can
(hang out with higher achievers)
- Wake up early everyday
- Read daily

"It doesn't matter how fast you can go, it doesn't matter
how much passion you have, and it doesn't matter how
much energy you put into something. If you don't have a
vision and clarity on the destination you want to reach,
you'll simply never get there."
—*Dean Graziosi*

As you look at your life, I highly encourage you to refer
back to this book and look for ideas that can help you get
centered and focused. I also recommend having your two-
minute story ready, as you never know who you might meet
and when. On top of that, understanding your two-minute
story can help you reach your goals and dreams.

This story is simple, and it revolves around where you
came from, where are you now, and where are you going.
For example, my two-minute story is: I was born and raised
in Mexico City to a poor family, having to work as a child
to survive. I was an immigrant to this great nation,
educated, and am now a business owner. I'm looking to
further expand my knowledge to inspire and help others,
make a difference in their lives, help them get motivated
and also be financially stable enough to provide for my
family.

With regard to helping others, I have initiated an
accountability group where the main objective is to focus
on several major actions and create an atmosphere around
them. These actions are wins, losses, fixes, aha moments,

feedback, and coaching. If you are interested in being part of this group, please contact me at facebook.com/cesar. espino.1297.

Last but not least, I recommend connecting yourself to a higher power, whether God, Mother Nature, or whatever or whomever you believe in. This is part of your daily rituals, and it can be accomplished through prayer, appreciation, meditation, or just being in a silent place to think, reflect, and be. Be grateful, appreciate life, connect with a power greater than you, and have faith that no one and nothing can stop you from reaching your set plans.

2016 changed me. 2017 broke me. 2018 opened my eyes. And in 2019 I'm coming back. You are next!

Thank you for taking the time to read this book. I am honored to have provided some fundamental ideas that can positively affect your life. Just as my life has changed over the years, I want to leave you with the reminder that no matter what, no one can stop you. You can achieve anything you want as long as you are certain, clear, and act now.

"I will do what it takes to make it happen before dying! And I will not die not doing what it takes to make it happen!"
—*Cesar R. Espino*

ACKNOWLEDGMENTS

First and foremost, no book is completed without the support and help of those with whom you have surrendered yourself. I would like to take the opportunity to thank my parents for always believing in me and giving me the support I need.

My daughter, Daisy Espino, who has stood by me through thick and thin during the creation of this book, and through many other experiences in my personal and professional life.

I also want to give a special thanks to few of my good friends who, no matter what, believed in me when others did not believe or see my potential.

This book is very special to me, and I really want to acknowledge all those people who saw me struggle, grow, and further inspire me to write and make this dream come true. Last but not least, I am grateful for the opportunities and the life that I was given. I am grateful for having gone through so many challenges and for now having the opportunity to share them with you to inspire you to reach for the sky.

"Whether you think you can, or you think you can't…you are right"
–*Henry Ford*

ABOUT THE AUTHOR

Cesar R. Espino is a naturalized US Citizen currently residing in Los Angeles, California. A full-time entrepreneur with an intensive background in business, he holds a Masters of Business Administration as well as a Bachelor of Science in Information Technology.

His passion is motivation, and his drive to succeed goes back to his roots. Born in Mexico City into a society of poverty and very little hope, it took years for him to recognize that a larger purpose had been set in front of him, one that he would chase for the rest of his life.

As a child, Cesar was giving and caring, saving the very few pesos he was given (and oftentimes with no money whatsoever for weeks) only to give them to others for enjoyment. As an immigrant to the US, there were many challenges to overcome. Although migrating to the US is now recognized as a life-changing event, at that time Cesar did not see the opportunity and only faced humiliation and challenges that came from not fitting in with a new culture and society. The primary challenges were acclimating to his new world, adjusting to a culture comprised of multiple backgrounds and ethnicities, and simply wanting to fit in when the main barrier was communication.

As a young adult, Cesar worked his way up the ladder in the logistics industry, holding multiple management positions with major worldwide companies. He had the opportunity to travel all over the world and see firsthand the different cultures and struggles taking place in those locations. With a passion for becoming more, bringing value, taking life to the next level, and leaving a legacy, his major focuses are self-development, building relationships, helping others, and creating a business empire.

Some of the key elements of his philosophy are based on mindset shifts, mentoring, and surrounding oneself with the right type of people.

facebook.com/cesar.espino.1297